RISKY RADICALS

A Study on Fulfilling God's Plan for Your Life.

RISKY RADICALS

A Study on Fulfilling God's Plan for Your Life.

STEVE HILL

ARDENT
P R E S S

A Heartland Ministry Series Publication

TABLE OF CONTENTS

INTRODUCTION

I have chosen to follow with a nautical theme throughout this book. Read on and you'll see why.

The Christian life is an incredible journey filled with mountaintop experiences, sunny skies and tremendous blessings. But the journey is also filled with deep valleys, stormy days and great battles along the way.

One of the most important keys to living victoriously as a believer and to fulfilling the plan of God for your life is *to keep moving forward*. God is always trying to move His people forward, but the tendency for most is to want to park it right where we are.

Do you know what happens when you park? You develop what I call "spiritual barnacles." Barnacles are crustaceans that attach themselves to the hull of ships whenever a ship sits still. These barnacles slow the ship down, requiring it to expend great amounts of energy and fuel just to keep moving forward. Once attached, they require a lot of money and considerable effort to remove.

My friend, there's an important spiritual lesson for us to learn here. You can't afford to coast along in a form of 'comfortable Christianity' or to plateau in your spiritual walk. Why? Because the barnacles of hell will attach themselves to you when you sit still. They'll slow you down in your Christian walk. They'll cost you, and if not dealt with, they'll defeat you.

The way to keep these barnacles from attaching themselves to you is *to keep going forward as a Christian*. How do you move forward? By continually pursuing the Lord, by aligning yourself with His priorities, and by following His plan for your life rather than your own. That's what this study, *Risky Radicals*, is all about.

The Lord gave me the material you are about to study while I was on my knees before Him in prayer. I knew at the time that it was a word to help prepare the Body of Christ both individually and corporately for the days that lie before us.

Even now, I sense the urgency of the Holy Spirit. There's a divine calling upon this generation of believers and we must answer that call. We have a God-given responsibility to rise up and make a difference in our world. We, like Esther, have been called to the kingdom "for such a time as this."

I believe with all my heart that the greatest revival the world has ever seen is on the horizon. It will be marked with millions of salvations, and unprecedented days of signs and wonders, miracles and healings.

The Lord is searching the earth for those who want to make a difference in this world. The most incredible journey awaits those who will answer His call, step out of the boat, and determine to do something great with their lives for God.

Risky Radicals will inspire and challenge you to rise up and answer that call.

STEVE HILL
Senior Pastor
Heartland Fellowship Church

RISKY ~

a factor that involves exposure
to uncertain hazard or danger

RADICAL ~

one who advocates extreme measures;
a person who overturns and changes
the present state of things

RISKY RADICAL ~

one who is willing to expose himself
to hazard or danger in order to
make a change in his world

Sail The Seven C's

Lesson 1

A LONG TIME AGO, SAILORS WOULD TALK ABOUT SAILING THE SEVEN seas. If you asked one of these sailors to tell you about his life on the sea, he'd share fascinating tales of adventure, and chilling accounts of danger and perilous storms.

The Christian life is much like the journeys of these sailors of old. Imagine going from one seaport to another. Between those two ports are various seas that you must cross to your reach your final destination. Before you were saved, you were anchored to the port of hell. As a Christian, you've departed from the port of hell where you once were docked, and now you're heading to the port of heaven.

Using a play on words, in this first lesson we're going to cover the "Seven C's" of Christianity that each of us must sail across in order to one day arrive at the harbor of heaven.

First Things First

Nobody begins a voyage in the middle of the ocean. You must begin at the beginning. Start at the starting point. Pull up anchor at the dock. We all know that. Yet many try to start their journey as a Christian in the middle of the ocean. They get launched on a calm day and are given the impression that Christianity is smooth, easy sailing. But when the storms of life come, they often end up shipwrecked because they didn't properly come into Christianity and take the steps that we're going to cover in this lesson.

My friend, I've been around long enough to know that there's a place you start and a place you finish. If you want to finish, you must start at the beginning and cover all the steps in-between. Understanding these steps will help keep you on course and also enable you to help others reach the harbor of heaven.

To set sail in Christianity:

1. You must first experience the CONVICTION of the Holy Ghost.

Just as a ship can't set sail without first pulling up anchor, neither can you set sail in Christianity without first experiencing the conviction of the Holy Ghost. Conviction is the point of embarkation. It's the place you pull up anchor.

'To convict' means 'to be found guilty.' Jesus said that the Holy Spirit is the One who convicts us and finds us guilty of sin.

> *But I tell you the truth, it is to your advantage that I go away; for if I do not go away, the Helper shall not come to you; but if I go, I will send Him to you. And He, when He comes, will convict the world concerning sin, and righteousness, and judgment.* (John 16:7-8)

> Many try to start their journey as a Christian in the middle of the ocean.

I remember a time when God had absolutely no place in my life. I could steal, do drugs, break the law, and hurt people with my words and actions, and I could have cared less. I had no conscience about it. My heart was so hard, that my sin didn't bother me at all. Do you remember such a time in your life?

Thank God, the Holy Ghost begins to work on our sinful, stony hearts while we're unsaved. He convicts us of sin and our need for Christ. We begin to feel guilty.

This may be elementary, but it's so important for you to grasp. If you don't know you're sick, you won't seek to get well. If you don't perceive you have a problem, you'll never search out the answer. If you don't realize you have a desperate need, you'll never seek to have it filled. If you don't realize you're lost, how can you be found? If you don't realize you're a sinner, how can you receive Jesus Christ as your Savior?

Let me explain it another way. Jesus came to save us from our sin. But if we're never convicted of our sin and our need for forgiveness – if we don't feel the weight of our sin – if we don't realize that because we've violated God's law, we're doomed to spend eternity in hell – if we don't realize that we're sinners in need of a Savior – then how can we be saved? Conviction then, is necessary to bring us to Christ.

This brings me to a problem that's troubling me as a man of God. I'm deeply concerned about what's being preached in pulpits throughout America today. Most preaching brings very little conviction or repentance these days. Instead, much of the focus is upon making people feel good. My friend, Jesus didn't die on the cross to make us feel good. He shed His blood to take away the sin of the world.

Instead of giving people what they *really* need to deal with the *sin* in their lives, the message of the day is, "God understands what you're going through. He will help you…"

Jesus *did* help us two thousand years ago – with nails, spikes, horrific stripes on His back, a crown of thorns, and a spear thrust through His side. Yes, He did help us and He *will* help us. But the real issue is, what are *you* going to do with the help He's already provided through the cross?

Let's look to the Word to get a better understanding of the purpose and power of conviction.

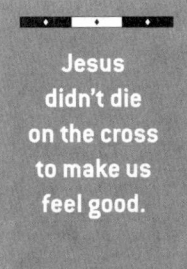

Jesus didn't die on the cross to make us feel good.

David Under Conviction

During the time when David was fleeing for his life from Saul, there was an incident where Saul entered a pitch-dark cave in search of a private bathroom. He had no idea that David, the very man he was trying to kill, was also in that cave. David could have easily killed Saul but instead, he cut off a small piece of Saul's garment without Saul even realizing it.

When he did that, the Bible tells us, *"David's heart smote him, because he had cut off Saul's skirt"* (I Samuel 24:4-6). David was convicted in his heart for cutting Saul's robe.

Another time, we read about David's deep conviction and prayer of repentance when he was confronted by the prophet Nathan for his sin of adultery and murder.

> *Have mercy on me, O God, according to your unfailing love; according to your great compassion blot out my transgressions.*
>
> *Wash away all my iniquity and cleanse me from my sin. For I know my transgressions and my sin is always before me...*
>
> *Create in me a pure heart, O God, and renew a steadfast (right) spirit within me. Do not cast me from your presence or take your Holy Spirit from me.*
>
> *Restore to me the joy of your salvation...*
> *(Psalm 51:1-2,10,12a)*

Do you see through David's life the purpose and power of conviction? *Conviction* led David to *repentance. Repentance* led to God's *mercy* and *forgiveness.* Think about it. Without conviction, David wouldn't have repented. Without repentance, he would not have received forgiveness.

This is why conviction is so important!

On The Day of Pentecost

The last thing Jesus told His disciples before He ascended into heaven was that they would receive power when the Holy Spirit came upon them and as a result, they would be His witnesses to the ends of the earth (Acts 1:8).

Indisputably and undeniably, they received that power when the Holy Spirit came upon them on the Day of Pentecost. A huge crowd gathered to see what all the commotion was about. Then Peter boldly preached Christ to the multitude. Look what happened.

> *Peter's words convicted them deeply, and they said to him and to the other apostles, "Brothers, what should we do?"*   *(Acts 2:37, NLT)*

The NIV says, *"When the people heard this, they were cut to the heart."*

Peter replied,

> *"Repent, and be baptized every one of you in the name of Jesus Christ for the forgiveness of your sins. And you will receive the gift of the Holy Spirit. The promise is for you and your children and for all who are far off – for all whom the Lord our God will call." With many other words, he warned them; and he pleaded with them...*
> *(Acts 2:38-40a, NIV)*

Peter told them to repent and be baptized, and that they'd receive the Holy Spirit. Then he warned and pleaded with them.

Look at the results:

> *Those who accepted his message were baptized, and about three thousand were added to their number that day.*   *(Acts 2:38)*

17

Three thousand people were added to the Church in one day! What an awesome miracle! My friend, those three thousand people would not have repented had they not first experienced conviction!

The Philippian Jailer

In Acts 16, we read the account of Paul and Silas being thrown into jail because Paul had cast a demon out of a slave girl. After being severely beaten and flogged, they were thrust into a deep dungeon, with their feet in stocks.

Around midnight, as Paul and Silas were praying and singing hymns to the Lord, God sent a violent earthquake that shook the very foundations of the prison. Suddenly, the prison doors flew open and everybody's chains came loose. Thinking that the prisoners had all fled, the jailer drew his sword to kill himself. But Paul shouted, "Don't harm yourself! We're all here!" The jailer rushed in, fell trembling before Paul and Silas and asked, "Sirs, what must I do to be saved?"

God does the same thing today. Many times He orchestrates 'earthquakes' in people's lives to bring them to the place of conviction and the realization of their great need for Him.

An Ongoing Ministry Of The Holy Spirit

Friend, call it what you want: being troubled, pricked in heart, a rapidly pounding heart, the heebie-jeebies, nervous in church, a queasy feeling, unpeaceful, uncomfortable, agitated – whatever you may call it my friend, that's conviction.

> Conviction is a sign of His presence.

Conviction is not only an essential work of the Holy Spirit to bring us *to* Christ, but it's also an *ongoing* work of the Holy Spirit in the life of every Christian.

I thank God that today, thirty years after my conversion experience, when I do or say something that grieves the Holy Spirit, I feel it.

Let me share three reasons why conviction is good:

1. Conviction is a sign of His **presence.**

Conviction is an awesome, wonderful thing, my friend, because it's a sign of His presence. It's a sign that He's with you. That He's not left you. That's He's working in you.

> *Whither shall I go from thy spirit? Or whither shall I flee from thy presence? If I ascend up into heaven, thou art there: if I make my bed in hell, behold, thou art there. If I take the wings of the morning, and dwell in the uttermost parts of the sea; even there shall thy hand lead me, and thy right hand shall hold me.* (Psalm 139:7-10)

2. Conviction is a sign of His **patience.**

When I got saved, it was so serious. I was a burned-out drug addict, on my way to hell. But God delivered me. He set me free. He washed my sins away. Adopted me into His family. Wiped my slate clean. Put my name in His book of life. He did all that for me, not just so I could enjoy a good life and then go to heaven one day. No, He saved me for a purpose that goes way beyond me. And the same is true for you.

Yet many believers are so casual about their salvation. They plod along spiritually at a snail's pace, struggling for years with the same issues, the same sins, and the same problems. But that's not the life He's called us to live. He says to every single believer, "I've saved you and changed your life. Now do something. Get serious. Get the sin out of your life and become a soldier in My army. There's work to do. The time is short."

Thank God for His patience. The conviction of the Holy Spirit is proof that He's working with you, that He's not left you.

> *But thou, O Lord, art a God full of compassion, and gracious, longsuffering, and plenteous in mercy and truth.* *(Psalm 86:15)*

Have you ever come down from a mountaintop experience with God only to face the biggest trial of your life? Or have you ever made great progress spiritually, and then you blew it? That's because of flesh. Thank God that when you blew it, you were convicted. You felt guilty. You felt awful.

Many treat conviction lightly. But remember, just because God is silent doesn't mean that He's not taking notes. And just because He's patient, doesn't mean you have all the time in the world. The Bible warns us that *His Spirit will not always strive with man.* (Genesis 6:3)

His patience and forbearance is there for a reason: to lead us to repentance and a life of faithful obedience.

3. Conviction is proof God has a **purpose.**

Is the Holy Spirit convicting you of something? I have good news. His conviction is proof that He has a purpose for your life! That He's not given up on you. That He has a plan and a destiny for you to fulfill.

> *The Lord is not slack concerning His promise, as some men count slackness; but is longsuffering to usward, not willing that any should perish, but that all should come to repentance.* *(2 Peter 3:9)*

Remember what happened to Saul of Tarsus on the road to Damascus? A light shined from heaven. He was blinded and knocked to the ground. Then he heard a voice say, "Saul, Saul, why do you persecute Me?" Saul responded saying, "Who are You, Lord?" "I am Jesus whom you persecute." The Lord then told him, "I have appeared unto you for this purpose, to make you a minister and a witness..." (see Acts 26:15-18)

God's desire and will is that all be saved. The fact that we experience the conviction of the Holy Spirit is proof that He has a purpose for our lives.

Three Responses To Conviction

There are three responses to the conviction of the Holy Spirit. We find these three responses when Paul preached Christ and the resurrection to the people of Athens.

> *And when they heard of the resurrection of the dead, some mocked: and others said, We will hear thee again of this matter...A few men became followers of Paul and believed.* (Acts 17:32,34)

1) Some will mock. 2) Some will procrastinate. 3) Some will believe.

Remember, these are boats that are parked in hell, and somebody is trying to help them pull up their anchors. But some aren't so quick to want their anchors to be pulled up.

Some will mock. If they mocked Jesus and Paul, they will also mock you.

Some will procrastinate. The sad thing about procrastinators is that they don't always get a second chance. The next day, when the procrastinators went to hear Paul preach a second time, Paul was gone.

Some believed. It's so important to respond quickly to the conviction of the Lord. Today is the day of salvation.

Here's something important to understand. Conviction doesn't save you. It's simply the catalyst that causes you to pull up anchor

> Conviction doesn't save you; it's simply the catalyst that causes you to pull up anchor out of the harbor of hell.

out of the harbor of hell. Once the rope of conviction is pulled up, the boat begins to shimmy and rock, you start floating, and into the second "C" of Christianity you go.

To set sail in Christianity:

2. You must experience genuine CONVERSION.

After the "C" of conviction, you must next experience genuine conversion. This means that you change, that you turn around. It means that you're headed in one direction (Satan/hell), but then you do a 180-degree turn and now you're going the opposite direction (Jesus/heaven). It means that you've turned from your past life and you're now going in a different direction. Let's look at some New Testament conversions.

Saul of Tarsus

I believe in rapid conversions. Paul's conversion is one such example. He was converted on the road to Damascus when he was knocked to the ground, saw a blinding light and heard a voice speak from heaven. In just a matter of seconds, he went from persecuting Christians to calling Jesus, "Lord."

> And Saul, yet breathing out threatenings and slaughter against the disciples of the Lord, went unto the high priest, And desired of him letters to Damascus to the synagogues, that if he found any of this way, whether they were men or women, he might bring them bound unto Jerusalem.
> And as he journeyed, he came near Damascus: and suddenly there shined round about him a light from heaven: And he fell to the earth, and heard a voice

I believe in rapid conversions.

saying unto him, Saul, Saul, why persecutest thou me? And he said, Who art thou, Lord?

And the Lord said, I am Jesus whom thou persecutest: it is hard for thee to kick against the pricks.

And he trembling and astonished said, Lord, what wilt thou have me to do? And the Lord said unto him, Arise, and go into the city, and it shall be told thee what thou must do.   *(Acts 9:1-5)*

The Ethiopian Eunuch

In Acts 8:35-38, Philip preached Jesus to the Ethiopian Eunuch. The eunuch was converted and immediately baptized.

Then Philip opened his mouth, and began at the same scripture, and preached unto him Jesus. And as they went on their way, they came unto a certain water: and the eunuch said, See, here is water; what doth hinder me to be baptized?

And Philip said, If thou believest with all thine heart, thou mayest. And he answered and said, I believe that Jesus Christ is the Son of God.

And he commanded the chariot to stand still: and they went down both into the water, both Philip and the eunuch; and he baptized him.

The Day of Pentecost

About 3,000 believed on Christ and were baptized in responses to Peter's preaching on the day of Pentecost.

So those who accepted his message were baptized, and that day about 3,000 people were added to them.   *(Acts 2:41)*

Nicodemus

Nicodemus was a man of the law. He was a religious leader in Israel. The fact that he came to Jesus secretly by night indicates that he had pulled up his anchor. He was under conviction.

> *There was a man of the Pharisees, named Nicodemus, a ruler of the Jews: The same came to Jesus by night, and said unto him, Rabbi, we know that thou art a teacher come from God: for no man can do these miracles that thou doest, except God be with him.* *(John 3:1-3)*

Notice what Jesus did. He brought Nicodemus from the known to the unknown.

> *Jesus answered and said unto him, Verily, verily, I say unto thee, Except a man be born again, he cannot see the kingdom of God.*
> *Nicodemus saith unto him, How can a man be born when he is old? can he enter the second time into his mother's womb, and be born?*
> *Jesus answered, Verily, verily, I say unto thee, Except a man be born of water and of the Spirit, he cannot enter into the kingdom of God. That which is born of the flesh is flesh; and that which is born of the Spirit is spirit. Marvel not that I said unto thee, Ye must be born again. The wind bloweth where it listeth, and thou hearest the sound thereof, but canst not tell whence it cometh, and whither it goeth: so is every one that is born of the Spirit.*
> *Nicodemus answered and said unto him, How can these things be? Jesus answered and said unto him, Art thou a master of Israel, and knowest not these things?* *(John 3:4-10)*

Test the waters to see where people are at before you pray the sinner's prayer with them.

History records that Nicodemus became a powerful follower of Jesus Christ. In fact, while all of Jesus' disciples were fleeing the crucifixion, Nicodemus showed up with seventy-five pounds of burial herbs and spices to help bury Jesus. Why? Because Nicodemus had been converted!

Test The Waters

Always remember, conviction comes before conversion. When I lead people to Jesus, I wait for them to be convicted. My friend, when you tell people about Jesus, test the waters to see where they're at before you pray the sinner's prayer with them.

Some people will say the prayer with you just to get you off their back. I know. We used to do just that at rescue missions back before I got saved. You'd always have to listen to someone preach before they'd let you eat. I remember two guys who sat in front of me at one rescue mission. One turned to the other and said, "Hey Jack. I got 'saved' yesterday. You do it today..." Why? Because as soon as someone went forward, everyone got to eat.

If you lead people to Jesus without them being ready, you have violated them spiritually rather than converting them. The fruit must be ripe before you pick it.

To sail in Christianity:

3. You must be CONVINCED that Jesus Christ has become your personal friend and Savior.

Romans 8:16 tells us that *the Spirit itself beareth witness with our spirit, that we are the children of God...*

When I got saved, I knew that I knew I was saved. No one could convince me that I wasn't saved. Why? Because a preacher told me I was saved? No, because I knew in my spirit that I was saved.

Now I'm not saying that I knew in my spirit that I was perfect. When I got saved, I still looked like a sinner. And it took several months to get a lot of the junk out of my life. But I was convinced in my heart that I was saved.

Ephesians 1:13-14 tells us what happens when we get saved,

> *After that ye believed, ye were sealed with that Holy Spirit of promise, which is the earnest of our inheritance until the redemption of the purchased possession, unto the praise of his glory.*

We're sealed with the Holy Ghost. He begins to speak to us and deal with our hearts. Now He says, "You belong to Jesus. Your life is not your own."

But the problem with many people is that they try to start Christianity in the middle of the ocean. You can't just say, "Well, I think I'll be a Christian," and then just join a church roll and you're 'in.' No, you must first be convicted, then converted, and then convinced that Jesus is your friend and Savior.

Once you're convinced that Jesus has become your personal friend and Savior, you're not just setting sail anymore. Now you're sailing.

To sail in Christianity:

4. You must undergo CHANGE in your human nature.

Tears are a sign of a godly man.

At this point, you are no longer setting sail in Christianity. Now you are sailing. When you become a Christian, you change. If there's no change, then you're still parked in the harbor of hell. 2 Corinthians 5:17 tells us, *"if any man be in Christ, he is a new creature: old things are passed away; behold, all things are become new."*

It doesn't say, "behold, *some* things become new." It says *"all things are become new."* Husbands, that means when you tell your wife that God's moving in your life, she's going to look for change in your behavior. It's not how much you read your Bible. It's what you do *after* you read your Bible. Young person, when you tell your mom and dad that God really touched you in a youth service, your parents are going to look for changes in your attitude and behavior. Ezekiel 36:26-27 says,

> *A new heart also will I give you, and a new spirit will I put within you: and I will take away the stony heart out of your flesh, and I will give you a heart of flesh. And I will put my spirit within you, and cause you to walk in my statues, and ye shall keep my judgments, and do them.*

Let me share a very personal story from my own life to illustrate this change of heart. When my father died, I was just sixteen years old. I was unsaved. As my family mourned and wept at his funeral, I didn't shed a single tear. I was stoned out of my mind. I remember standing over my Dad's casket, looking at him for the last time. I felt nothing. In a casual, flippant kind of way, I said, "good riddance," and walked away. That was it. No emotion. No sorrow. Nothing. My natural father had died and my heart was as hard as rock. I could have cared less.

But years later when I got saved, one of the first things I desired to do was to get to know my Dad again. Of course, I couldn't. He was dead. So I'd ask my Mom about him. I asked if he had ever had any religious experiences and she said, "No." I said, "You never saw Dad read the Bible?" "No." "You never heard him pray?" "No." I remember weeping and weeping over the fact that Dad never embraced Jesus. Before I was saved, my heart towards my dad was as hard as rock. But when I became a Christian, I wept, grieved, and mourned over him.

Why? Because Jesus changed my heart. He put a new heart in me. He changed me. I'm not a proud man anymore. I'm a broken man. I'm a different man. I became a weeper, and I've wept for the last thirty years. Tears, my friend, are a sign of a godly man. If Jesus wept, so can you.

When you become a Christian, you're new. God begins to do a mighty work in you. You change. A thief quits stealing. A drunkard quits drinking. A gambler quits gambling. A drug addict drops his needle. A curser stops cursing. A wife abuser stops abusing. A rebellious man or woman becomes soft and pliable.

When was the last time you thanked Him for saving you? My friend, this is something you should do every single day!

To make progress sailing in Christianity:

5. You must be CONSUMED with His Spirit.

I thank God for spiritual experiences. One-time spiritual experiences are fine, but always remember—an experience won't cause you to grow or progress as a Christian.

Follow the bloodline from Genesis to Revelation, and then go back and follow the Spirit. If you start with Genesis–the beginning of time–and go all the way to the end of the book, you will see these lines of the Spirit of God throughout the entire Bible. The same Holy Spirit who convicted people in the book of Genesis during the days of Noah ("My Spirit will not always strive with man," Genesis 6:3) is convicting people throughout the whole Bible, all the way to the book of Revelation.

> An experience won't cause you to grow or progress as a Christian.

If you had an experience back in 1972, that's great. But I want to know if you've had an experience lately? Do you still speak in tongues? Have you grown in the Lord? Do you have power to be a witness?

And be not drunk with wine, wherein

is excess; but be filled with the Spirit (Ephesians 5:18)

To be filled with the Spirit means that we're totally supplied, filled up, overflowing, and consumed with the Spirit of God. This is not just a one-time experience.

To maintain your course in Christianity:

6. You must align yourself with the CHALLENGE of the Great Commission.

There are three questions in life everyone should be able to answer: *who am I, why am I here,* and *where am I going.* I know the answers to those questions. I'm heading to the harbor of heaven and the way for me to get there is by obedience.

My friend, the Holy Spirit is the One who blows the sails that lead you safely to that harbor. To stay on course, you must focus on what He's commanded us to do. Jesus said in Matthew 28:19-20,

> *Go ye therefore, and teach all nations, baptizing them in the name of the Father, and of the Son, and of the Holy Ghost.*

He also said,

> *Go ye into all the world, and preach the gospel to every creature. He that believeth and is baptized shall be saved; but he that believeth not shall be damned.* (Mark 16:15-18)

There's nothing complicated about that. God's priority is always SOULS. That's why aligning yourself with the challenge of the Great Commission will help you stay on course.

But just as boats often drift, so do many Christians. Instead of staying on track with the Great Commission, they drift totally off course and often end up shipwrecked because of some tangent or wind of doctrine that they picked up along the way.

A few years ago, we had plans to hold a mass crusade in London at Prince Albert Hall. The pastors in London had been planning the event for a year and a half, and had spent over $25,000 on publicity. They had all the advertising printed up. It was all systems go for this powerful, evangelistic event.

But I got a call from one of the pastors who was heading up the crusade and he said, "Steve, the pastors who were once interested in winning souls in London have now picked up on the latest teaching from America, and they're no longer interested in having an evangelistic crusade. Instead, they want prosperity preachers to come in and teach. What should we do?" I said, "Cancel the crusade." The pastors who had backed out were on the planning committee. Think about it. Within a year and a half, this group of pastors had drifted from going after souls to following after prosperity.

The same type of thing happened in Wales. We held a crusade in Wales a few years ago and saw over 1,000 conversions. Some pastors said, "We've never seen a move of God like this. It reminds us of all the stories from the Welsh Revival back at the turn of the last century." So they invited me to return for a centennial celebration of the Welsh Revival. Do you know what happened? Seventy-five percent of all the pastors that were on board when we held the first Wales Crusade were a few years later operating 'seeker friendly' churches. They had totally drifted off course and weren't interested in going after souls.

The Bible says that we are to *seek first the kingdom of God and His righteousness and all these things shall be added unto you* (Matthew 6:33).

He will never lead you apart from the Word.

To make sure your ship cruises straight across the ocean to the harbor of heaven, stay focused upon the Great Commission. When you wake up each morning, ask, "Jesus, what do You want me to do? What am I going to do today and how will it determine eternity in other people's lives?"

As you align yourself with His priorities, you will see His hand of blessing upon your life.

To make progress sailing in Christianity:

7. You must exercise the daily COMFORT of the Holy Spirit.

As you sail across the sea of Christianity, you will encounter storms that buffet and bob your boat like a cork in the ocean. That's why you need the tender presence of the Holy Spirit in your life. He's the One who will comfort, guide, and keep you on the straight course to heaven, my friend.

Jesus told us,

> *And I will pray the Father and he shall give you another Comforter, that he may abide with you forever.*
> *(John 14:16)*

The word "Comforter" means "One called along side to help." Holy Spirit will come along side and help you. How? As the Spirit of Truth, He's going to lead you into truth. Jesus said of Him,

> *Howbeit when he, the Spirit of truth, is come, he will guide you into all truth: for he shall not speak of himself; but whatsoever he shall hear, that shall he speak: and he will shew you things to come.   (John 16:13)*

Let me give you an example of how He guides you into all truth. Have you ever heard a strange teaching that made you feel uneasy? More than likely, that uneasy feeling wasn't 'just you', but rather

> **Begin to acknowledge the presence of the Holy Spirit in your life every day.**

the Spirit of God in you. He was cautioning you. What was being taught wasn't in line with the Word.

This is why it's so important to fill yourself with the Word, because the Holy Spirit will never lead you apart from the Word. Fill yourself with the Word and learn to listen to the Holy Spirit. He's the One who's going to teach you. He's the One who's going to whisper in your ear and say, "Susie, you're a little off course. Go back this way a bit. There you go. You're right on course again."

My friend, there's nothing like the sweet presence of the Holy Spirit. If you love the Lord with all your heart, soul, and strength, then He's with you. But I encourage you to deepen your relationship with Him. Begin to acknowledge the presence of the Holy Spirit in your life every day. As Proverbs 3:6 tells us, *In all your ways acknowledge Him, And He shall direct your paths.*

Staying The Course

Understanding the seven "C's" of Christianity will help you stay on course and eventually reach the harbor of heaven. But that's not all. This understanding will also enable you to help others.

Learn to locate where people are and how they got there. When I meet people who have been shipwrecked in Christianity, I'll often ask them, "Would you explain to me how you came to the Lord?" Often they will tell me that they've known the Lord all their life. Then I'll say, "Yes, but tell me, when did you *really* decide to follow Jesus?" Many times, they can't tell me the answer.

My friend, if they can't respond by saying something like, "When I was nineteen years, I really started following Jesus..." If they can't say, "I feel His presence, and when I'm doing wrong, He convicts me..." If they don't have those type of reference points, then go back to the beginning and take them through the first "C's" of Christianity by saying, "You know something,

Susie, why don't we ask the Lord to forgive us and repent of our sins right now? I want you to cry out to God right now. Let's start brand new..."

As you take them through the process, you're going to see them go all the way in their Christianity. Why? Because they started out right, and they have the proper foundation to steer their ship and stay on course.

Don't Get Too Comfortable

Now that you're safely in the boat and have set sail in Christianity, don't get too comfortable. The Lord is going to send some storms your way to cause you to step *out* of the boat, as we'll discuss in our next lesson.

Questions For Group Discussion

1. To set sail in Christianity, you must first experience the CONVICTION of the Holy Spirit.

    a. Describe the conviction of the Holy Spirit in your life prior to your conversion. _____

    _____

    _____

    _____

    _____

    b. What's the purpose of conviction? What does conviction signify?

    _____

    _____

    _____

    _____

    _____

    _____

2. Read Romans 10:13-15,

    For whosoever shall call upon the name of the Lord shall be saved. How then shall they call on him in whom they have not believed? and how shall they believe in him of whom they have not heard? and how shall they hear without a preacher? And how shall they preach, except they be sent? as it is written, How beautiful are the feet of them that preach the gospel of peace, and bring glad tidings of good things!

Discuss the importance of sharing the gospel in the following conversions:

    a.   The 3,000 on the Day of Pentecost (Acts 2:37-40)
    b.   The Philippian jailer (Acts 16)
    c.   Saul of Tarsus (Acts 9)
    d.   Your own salvation experience _____

_____

_____

_____

_____

3.   Read the following scriptures and discuss how they relate to the New Birth.

Therefore if any man be in Christ, he is a new creature: old things are passed away; behold, all things are become new.   (*2 Corinthians 5:17*)

A new heart also will I give you, and a new spirit will I put within you: and I will take away the stony heart out of your flesh, and I will give you an heart of flesh. And I will put my spirit within you, and cause you to walk in my statutes, and ye shall keep my judgments, and do them.   (*Ezekiel 36:26-27*)

    a.   What does it mean to be a new creature in Christ?

_____

_____

_____

_____

_____

b. How is this change in nature evidenced? _____

_____

_____

_____

_____

_____

_____

4. Discuss the ministry of the Holy Spirit in the life of the believer as it relates to:

a. Bringing CONVICTION (see John 16:8) _____

_____

_____

_____

_____

_____

_____

b. Being CONSUMED (filled) with the Spirit
    (see Ephesians 5:18-20) _____

_____

_____

_____

_____

_____

_____

c. Experiencing His daily COMFORT (see John 14:25-27)

_____

_____

_____

_____

_____

_____

Boat People

Lesson 2

HAVE YOU EVER HEARD THE SAYING, "I'D RATHER BE A WET WATER walker than a dry boat sitter"? Of course, that statement is referring to the miracle of Peter walking on the water. If you've been a Christian for any length of time, you've probably heard several sermons about that incredible event. I know I certainly have. But I don't recall ever hearing a message about the disciples who stayed *in* the boat on that stormy, history-making night.

I've studied this miracle in depth and do you know what I've discovered? There's just as much for us to learn from the disciples who stayed *in* the boat, as there is from Peter, who walked on the water.

Me, A Boat Person?

So which one best describes you? Are you a water walker like Peter, or a boat sitter like the rest of the disciples? Of course, you're probably thinking, "I'm more like Peter..." And maybe so. But if we're honest with ourselves, we'd admit that at times we've been boat people, too.

Think about it. If eleven out of the twelve disciples remained in the boat – men who walked with Jesus, experienced His miracles, and sat under His teaching...if eleven of Jesus' closest disciples stayed in the boat, where does that leave us?

"But I Love My Boat..."

The fact is, the majority of Christians are content living in the security of their own little boat. You may be thinking, "But Steve, I love God. I go to church. Pay tithes. Take care of my family. Life is good. I like my comfortable, secure boat. What's wrong with that?"

My friend, Jesus didn't die on the cross so you could enjoy a comfortable life on earth and then go to heaven someday. He died on the cross to pay the price for your sin and the sins of the world. As a Christian, your life is not your own. You belong to God.

You're here on the earth for a reason – a divine purpose that is deep in the heart of every believer. Yet sadly, the majority of Christians live their entire lives barely scratching the surface of what God has for them. This is in part due to what I call a *boat people mentality*.

When the Lord gave me the message *Boat People*, I saw myself through the mirror of His Word, and I was challenged. As you delve into this lesson, you, too, are going to see yourself and be challenged in your walk with Him. And that's a good thing.

I'm so thankful that over the years the Lord has put me around men and women of God who challenge me. I *love* to be around people who live holy, who believe God's Word, and who step out to do the impossible. They dream big dreams for God and say stuff like, "We need to get the Gospel into every Arabic nation of the world through television..." "How can we do this?" "I don't know, but somehow it's got to happen. Let's start walking out here..." They step out into uncharted waters, and WHAM - God performs a miracle and makes a way.

> The majority of Christians live their entire lives barely scratching the surface of what God has for them.

That's exactly what happened to a good friend of mine from Sweden, Ulf Eckman. He planted a church in Uppsala, Sweden that today numbers in the thousands. But back when he first started the church, he received tremendous opposition. He was smeared by the press. He was threatened, branded as a heretic, and his ministry was denounced as a cult. In the midst of this fierce opposition, the Lord told him to build a sanctuary that would hold 5,000 people – at a time when he had a mere 200 members in his church! Imagine that. In the natural, that's crazy. It doesn't make sense.

It reminds me of Noah. One day God spoke to him and said, "Noah, I want you to build an ark that's big enough to house every species of animals because I'm going to cause it to rain..." "Okay God. I've never seen an ark before. It's never rained before so I'm not exactly sure what rain is. But You just tell me what to do and I'll do it." (Genesis 6-7)

That's what Ulf did. He stepped out and obeyed God, while people mocked him and falsely accused him. But he kept on and he built that 5,000 seat sanctuary. The story doesn't end there. While he was building the sanctuary (remember, his church only had 200 members), the Lord spoke to him one day. "Ulf." "Yes, Lord?" "I want you to plant 1,000 churches in Russia, and I want you to do it now, while you are building your 5,000-seat church in Sweden." "Okay, Lord. Whatever You say, I'll do."

Ulf didn't have the capability or the resources to plant *10* churches in Russia, let alone *1,000* churches. But that didn't deter him. There was a need. God had spoken. So he said, "Yes," without question, and without arguing with God about why it couldn't be done. A few days later, a man from Russia came into his office and gave him a huge train. Do you know what Ulf did with that train? He used it to plant those churches throughout Russia. Everywhere the train stopped, they planted a church. 1,000 of them! While in the middle of a major building program at his own church in Sweden! Sound insane? To boat people, it *is* insane. But to a water walker like Ulf, his willingness to get out of the boat produced a tremendous miracle that reaped thousands upon thousands of souls getting saved! Today, the church he planted in Sweden holds 8,000 people! But what if Ulf had not been willing to get out of the boat and plant those 1,000 churches in Russia? Do you think God would have blessed Ulf's church in Sweden the way that He did? I think not.

What's To Learn From Boat People?

So what's to learn from the disciples who stayed in the boat? We'll get to that, but first we need to look at what happened just *before* that stormy night. Earlier that day, a multitude had followed Jesus to a remote place where He taught them and healed the sick. The hour got late and the people had no food to eat. They were in a remote place – not exactly within walking distance of your favorite fast food restaurant, you might say.

But Jesus had compassion on the people. He didn't want them to faint with hunger on their journey home, so He performed an awesome miracle: He fed over five thousand people with just five loaves of bread and two fish (see Matthew 14:13-21)! What an amazing miracle!

But Jesus didn't give the disciples the chance to bask in the afterglow of the miracle. The Bible says that immediately after the feeding of the five thousand, He forced the disciples to get into a boat and sail away without Him, while He dismissed the people. Here's where our story about boat people begins.

> *And straightway Jesus constrained his disciples to get into a ship, and to go before him unto the other side, while he sent the multitudes away. And when he had sent the multitudes away, he went up into a mountain apart to pray: and when the evening was come, he was there alone. But the ship was now in the midst of the sea, tossed with waves: for the wind was contrary.*
>
> *And in the fourth watch of the night Jesus went unto them, walking on the sea. And when the disciples saw him walking on the sea, they were troubled, saying, "It is a spirit;" and they cried out for fear.*
>
> *But straightway Jesus spake unto them, saying, "Be of good cheer; it is I; be not afraid." And Peter answered him and said, "Lord, if it be thou, bid me come unto thee on the water."*

And he said, "Come."

And when Peter was come down out of the ship, he walked on the water, to go to Jesus. But when he saw the wind boisterous, he was afraid; and beginning to sink, he cried, saying, "Lord, save me." And immediately Jesus stretched forth his hand, and caught him, and said unto him, "O thou of little faith, wherefore didst thou doubt?"

And when they were come into the ship, the wind ceased. Then they that were in the ship came and worshipped him, saying, "Of a truth thou art the Son of God." (Matthew 14:22-33)

From The Mountain To The Valley

The disciples had just experienced a fantastic miracle – right before their very eyes. They watched Jesus multiply the fish and the loaves to feed 5,000 people. Can you imagine what they must have thought as they gave a piece of bread or fish to someone and it multiplied in their hands? Or maybe as they gave their last piece of fish away, they looked down at their plates and thought, "I know I just gave that last piece of fish away. How can there be fish in my basket?" They'd never seen anything like this before. No doubt, they were having a fun, mountain top experience with Jesus. At that moment, they must have felt like they were sitting on top of the world, and that anything was possible.

But oh how quickly they came off that mountain top experience only to find themselves in a fierce storm, battling for their lives. There's an important lesson for us to learn here, my friend. The Christian life is full of mountain top experiences followed by deep valleys. In a matter of moments, life can go from sunny skies to a fierce, dark storm. It's

> The Christian life is full of mountain top experiences followed by deep valleys. It's all in the Word.

all in the Word. The Lord put it in there so we'd learn not to be shaken when it happens to us.

Evidently, the disciples had not yet learned that lesson. Why was it that they were so shaken by the storm, especially since they had just experienced the miracle of the loaves and the fishes? Mark's account of this story sheds some light.

> *Then He got into the boat with them, and the wind ceased. They were completely astounded, because they did not understand about the loaves. Instead, their hearts were hardened.*
> *(Mark 6:51-52)*

Notice this. When Jesus came to the disciples walking on the water, they were completely astounded *because they did not understand about the loaves.* Why didn't they understand? The Bible says *because their hearts were hardened.* That means their minds were dull. It implies a "strange stupidity."

Present Storms Often Cloud Past Victories

My friend, this story is loaded with spiritual gems that apply to you and me. The disciples not considering the loaves and the fish represents how quick we are to forget the all-powerful hand of God. What do I mean by that? The feeding of the five thousand was a slow-paced, easy-to-handle, *daytime* miracle. The sun was shining. Jesus was in charge. He was with them. The disciples simply did what He told them to do. "Peter, feed this group of fifty." "Okay, Jesus." Piece of cake.

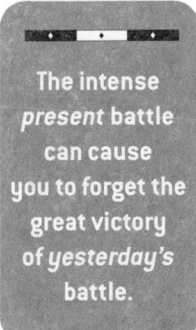

The intense *present* battle can cause you to forget the great victory of *yesterday's* battle.

But the disciples alone in a boat during a dangerous storm was an entirely different situation. Their lives were in danger. It was what I call a *nighttime* miracle, or a miracle that occurred during a dark hour or crisis.

Interestingly, this was the second time the disciples found themselves being tossed about by a severe storm on the Sea of Galilee. The first time, the Lord was asleep in the boat and the end result was the same. He rebuked the storm and stilled the waves. The disciples were astonished at His power. You can read the account in Matthew 8:23-27.

So why, when they encountered a storm the second time, did they fear for their lives instead of trusting in Jesus? They had experienced Jesus rebuking the storm and calming the sea once before. If Jesus did it once before, surely He could do it again...

There's a lesson to be learned here. Often our present, violent storms which represent our trials, blow away all the lessons learned from the previous storms. The intense, present battle that is raging can cause you to forget the great victory of yesterday's battle.

You must choose how you're going to react in the midst of the storm. Peter and the other eleven disciples all experienced the same wind and storm. Peter reacted one way; the eleven another. Peter walked on the water while the eleven sat in the boat and watched him.

This brings us to the first point we need to learn about Boat People.

Christians who choose to stay in the boat:

1. Can easily spend their entire lives watching others experience great moments with God.

The opportunity to walk on water was available to *all* of the disciples. But while the disciples were allowing the waves to bring *defeat*, Peter was allowing the waves to become a *street*.

What does this mean for you and for me? My friend, each one of us must make a choice when faced with adversity. Tests, trials, and

> While the disciples were allowing the waves to bring *defeat*, Peter was allowing the wave to become a *street*.

the storms of life come to everyone. But you alone decide how you're going to respond. No one can determine that for you.

If you choose to stay in the boat, you will forever stand on the sidelines watching others do great things for God. If you step out of the boat, you will experience great moments in God throughout your life.

A Shepherd Boy Rocks With Five Small Stones

Consider a similar Old Testament story of someone who did something extraordinary with his God while everyone else watched.

> *And David rose up early in the morning, and left the sheep with a keeper, and took, and went, as Jesse had commanded him; and he came to the trench, as the host was going forth to the fight, and shouted for the battle. For Israel and the Philistines had put the battle in array, army against army. And David left his carriage in the hand of the keeper of the carriage, and ran into the army, and came and saluted his brethren. And as he talked with them, behold, there came up the champion, the Philistine of Gath, Goliath by name, out of the armies of the Philistines, and spake according to the same words: and David heard them. And all the men of Israel, when they saw the man, fled from him, and were sore afraid.*
>
> *And the men of Israel said, "Have ye seen this man that is come up? Surely to defy Israel is he come up: and it shall be, that the man who killeth him, the king will enrich him with great riches, and will give him his daughter, and make his father's house free in Israel."*
>
> *And David spake to the men that stood by him, saying, "What shall be done to the man that killeth*

this Philistine, and taketh away the reproach from Israel? For who is this uncircumcised Philistine, that he should defy the armies of the living God?"

And the people answered him after this manner, saying, "So shall it be done to the man that killeth him." And Eliab his eldest brother heard when he spake unto the men; and Eliab's anger was kindled against David, and he said, "Why camest thou down hither? And with whom hast thou left those few sheep in the wilderness? I know thy pride, and the naughtiness of thine heart; for thou art come down that thou mightest see the battle."

And David said, "What have I now done? Is there not a cause?" And he turned from him toward another, and spake after the same manner: and the people answered him again after the former manner...

David said moreover, "The LORD that delivered me out of the paw of the lion, and out of the paw of the bear, he will deliver me out of the hand of this Philistine." And Saul said unto David, "Go, and the LORD be with thee."

(1 Samuel 17:20-30, 37)

Boy, talk about a bunch of boat people in the Old Testament. The whole army of Israel was paralyzed because of Goliath. Then a little shepherd boy named David comes to the battlefield one day and asks, "What's going on here?" "That big old giant out there is threatening to take everybody down. He's going to kill us all." David, who was just a kid, responded, "He's bugging you guys?" "Yeah, big time." David then said, "What's going to be done for the man who takes him down?" "That lucky guy gets to marry the king's daughter, have riches, and everything..." David begins to think to himself, "Hum. This sure beats tending sheep..."

You know the outcome. David boldly stepped out and took on Goliath. In the natural, he was crazy to do it. He seemed oblivious to what everyone else knew as obvious - there was no way he could defeat Goliath with five small stones and a slingshot. But he did! While the whole Israeli army – men of God in full armor with swords – sat back and watched.

This brings us to our next important lesson to be learned about boat people.

Christians who choose to stay in the boat:

2. Can easily spend their lives in paralyzing fear while watching others step out with reckless abandonment, motivated by overwhelming affection.

Why did David choose to take on Goliath when the odds were so greatly against him? Was it because he was a fierce warrior, or because he wanted the financial reward? Maybe it was because he wanted to marry the king's daughter. Perhaps. But I believe David's motivation went much deeper than that.

Let me explain it this way. If someone was to come against you, that's one thing. But if they came against your kids or your beloved spouse...boy, that's an entirely different matter. Touch your family – your loved ones – the apple of your eye – and that's like trying to take baby cubs away from a lioness.

That's what happened with David. The moment he heard Goliath blaspheme the Lord, he rose up to defend his God while the armies of Israel cowered in fear. Why? Because David was in love with his God!

What One Will Do For Love!

People debate what motivated Peter to step out of the boat on that stormy night. Many say it was his faith. Others, his personal prideful ambition. Some say it was just another one of his impulsive, spontaneous acts that flowed freely from his uninhibited, sanguine personality. I've studied this story over the years. I've even role-played, trying to imagine Peter's state of mind when Jesus came walking on the water.

Personally, I'm convinced that there wasn't a whole lot of faith involved in Peter's actions. But there is no doubt in my mind that Peter was infatuated with Jesus. He was one of those pillars who was with Jesus from the very beginning. He was the one who had declared, "Thou art the Christ, the Son of the living God...where else could we go?" He's the one who said, "Jesus, I'll die with you..." He's the one who sliced off Marcus' ear when Jesus was apprehended.

Yes, Peter was often reckless, and sometimes put his foot in his mouth, yet he had the right intentions. He loved Jesus with all his heart. I believe his affections toward Christ affected his actions and motivated him to step out of that boat. This overwhelming affection superseded his fear, his logic, and his negative circumstances. As a result, he did something no one else had ever done – he stepped out of the boat and walked on the water.

A boat person on the other hand, allows overwhelming fear to paralyze him. Consequently, he remains in the boat, unable to do anything worthwhile in life. My friend, if you're going to do anything significant in life, you'll have to get out of the boat.

Kathryn Kuhlman used to say that the only reason God used her in the powerful way that He did was because there was a man who said "no." I can just imagine what this man must have thought as he watched Kathryn experience great things with Jesus that he only wished he had the guts to step out and do. What was the difference between Kathryn and that man? I believe her overwhelming affection for Jesus motivated her to get out of the boat.

My love for the Lord has gotten me out of the boat on many occasions.

I'll say, "Jesus, is that You?" "It's Me, Steve. I Am that I Am..." Whoosh. "Here I come, Jesus. I love You. I want to be with You..."

> My love for the Lord has gotten me out of the boat on many occasions.

Remember the woman with the alabaster box? She entered a house where Jesus was eating with His disciples. She pressed past the opinions of all the boat people who were criticizing her. She took a very costly spikenard, broke it open on the ground and poured it upon His head. She loved on Him and adored Him while those around watched with indignation.

> *Now when Jesus was in Bethany, in the house of Simon the leper, There came unto him a woman having an alabaster box of very precious ointment, and poured it on his head, as he sat at meat. But when his disciples saw it, they had indignation, saying, "To what purpose is this waste? For this ointment might have been sold for much, and given to the poor."* (Matthew 26:6-9)

While the boat people saw the woman as one who interrupted them and wasted something precious, Jesus saw something totally different. He honored and spoke a heritage over her because of her selfless act of love and adoration for Him.

> *When Jesus understood it, he said unto them, "Why trouble ye the woman? for she hath wrought a good work upon me. For ye have the poor always with you; but me ye have not always. For in that she hath poured this ointment on my body, she did it for my burial. Verily I say unto you, Wheresoever this gospel shall be preached in the whole world, there shall also this, that this woman hath done, be told for a memorial of her."* (Matthew 26:10-13)

Sinking is awesome, because you get to experience the thrill of Jesus coming to your rescue!

What a heritage Jesus spoke over this woman! Wherever the Gospel would be preached throughout the world, what this woman had done would be told for a memorial to her. Here we are two thousand years later, recognizing her because she chose not to be a boat person, recognizing her for stepping out in reckless abandonment because of her love for Jesus.

Christians who choose to stay in the boat:

3. Never experience the thrill of having the rescuing hand of God take hold of them.

Sinking is awesome, my friend! Why? Because when you begin to sink, you get to experience the thrill of Jesus, like a knight in shining armor, coming to your rescue! That's what happened to Peter. When he began to sink, the Lord didn't rebuke him or let him drown. No, He graciously reached down and lifted Peter up.

He does the same thing with us. And do you know what the Lord says when you step out of the boat and begin to sink? "At least you tried!" As you go through experiences like this with the Lord, you develop confidence in His ability to keep you. The fear of failing diminishes. As a result, the next time you see the Lord walking towards you in the midst of the stormy sea, you'll get out of the boat!

When you let go of the world, your securities and your earthly wisdom, only then does God truly take hold of you. You will never experience Him *near* until your cry becomes *clear*. Take it from Peter. When he began to sink he didn't cry out, "Jesus, explain to me why I'm sinking...is there something wrong in my life?" Nope. He simply cried out, "Lord, save me!" How I love that. His cry was so simple and so clear.

The Step Of Obedience

Allow me to take a side journey for a moment. People sometimes come to my office and say, "Pastor Steve, everything is falling apart..." I let them talk for a few minutes, then I ask them, "Is there any habitual sin in your life?" If they say,

"No," then I'll ask, "Are you tithing?" Sometimes they'll look at me and say, "But I can't afford to tithe." Then we go back and discuss every one of their problems, and I can usually link almost every single one of them to disobeying God and His clear instructions in the Word.

What does this have to do with getting out of the boat? Everything, my friend. Because stepping out of the boat begins first and foremost with obeying the written Word of God and the prompting of the Holy Spirit. As you step out in obedience, Jesus will always come through for you.

On the other hand, I meet believers all the time who think they must have done something wrong every time they go through a test or trial. The tests and trials of life come to all of us. Jesus told us that when He said,

> *In the world, ye shall have tribulation. But be of good cheer, I have overcome the world.*
> *(John 16:33)*

Did you know that many of our trials come from an outside source? While we're not responsible for the trial coming, we *are* held accountable for how we behave during them. Look at the disciples. They weren't responsible for the storm that night. But they were responsible for how they behaved in the midst of the storm.

Look at what Thomas Edison had to say about the subject. "Many of life's failures are people who did not realize how close they were to success when they gave up." He knew from personal experience. One man came up to him and asked him, "What's it feel like to have failed two thousand times in trying to make a light bulb?" Edison replied, "Failed two thousand times? No, those weren't failures. I simply figured out two thousand ways that it couldn't be done…"

Sir Winston Churchill once said, "Success is the ability to go from one failure to another

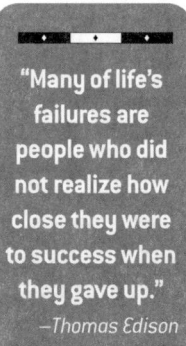

"Many of life's failures are people who did not realize how close they were to success when they gave up."
—Thomas Edison

with no loss of enthusiasm." If Peter was here, he would "amen" that statement because he went from one failure to another. His life was a link of failures, culminating at the time of Jesus' darkest hour when he cursed and denied the Lord. But in the end, Jesus restored him, and used him mightily in signs and wonders, and to preach that great message on the day of Pentecost.

Some people fail one time and give up. Because of a failure, they withdraw and sometimes live the rest of their lives never trying, never stepping out. That, my friend, is the mentality of a boat person. But you don't have to live this way. Let's learn from Peter's failures as well as his successes. He never gave up. When Jesus beckoned him, he stepped out. Whenever he faltered, Jesus rescued him. And what a mighty legacy he left for us to follow.

Perhaps you feel more like a boat person than a water walker right now. I have some good news for you.

Christians who choose to stay in the boat:

4. By virtue of association, reap the benefits of others.

Let's revisit the story of David and Goliath and see how the army of Israel reaped the benefits of David's great moment with God.

> And it came to pass, when the Philistine arose, and came and drew nigh to meet David, that David hasted, and ran toward the army to meet the Philistine. And David put his hand in his bag, and took thence a stone, and slang it, and smote the Philistine in his forehead, that the stone sunk into his forehead; and he fell upon his face to the earth.
>
> So David prevailed over the Philistine with a sling and with a stone, and smote the Philistine, and slew him; but there was no sword in the hand of David. Therefore David ran, and stood upon

the Philistine, and took his sword, and drew it out
of the sheath thereof, and slew him, and cut off
his head therewith.

And when the Philistines saw their champion
was dead, they fled.

And the men of Israel and of Judah arose,
and shouted, and pursued the Philistines, until thou
come to the valley, and to the gates of Ekron. And
the wounded of the Philistines fell down by the way
to Shaaraim, even unto Gath, and unto Ekron. And
the children of Israel returned from chasing after the
Philistines, and they spoiled their tents.

(I Samuel 17:48-53)

David slew the Philistine while all the "boat people" sat back and watched. As soon as he chopped off Goliath's head, the army of Israel rose up and pursued the Philistine army. They defeated their enemy that day AND came home with great spoils – all because a kid named David dared to step out and trust God!

Four Bold Lepers Who Blessed A City

In I Kings 6-7 we read about the time when the Syrian army besieged Samaria. For months, the Samaritans could not enter or leave their city. The famine was so severe that the Samaritans began to eat their own children. From the king to the lowliest peasant, the people were paralyzed with fear. Consequently, they sat and did nothing while their circumstances grew more and more desperate. *Boat People.*

One day, four lepers who were outside the city gate got tired of sitting around doing nothing. They figured that if they went into the city (Samaria - with the boat people), they would surely die because of the famine. On the other hand, if they went into the camp of the Syrians, maybe, somehow, they might find mercy and live. So off they went.

When they got to the camp of the Syrians, the place was empty. I mean, it was deserted with not a soul to be found. Do you know why? Because the Lord caused the Syrians to hear the great noise of horses and chariots coming upon them. Thinking they were under attack, the whole army fled in haste, leaving all of their food and belongings. Because of the bold action of four lepers, the city of Samaria was incredibly blessed!

If God could use four unclean, diseased lepers to so bless a city, then how much more can He use us – His children – who are willing to step out and follow Him?!

Peter Paves The Way

The good news is that every one of the disciples who stayed in the boat benefited from Peter's miracle that night. Consider this. Have you ever personally seen anyone walk on water? Probably not. Me neither. But the eleven who stayed in the boat were eyewitnesses of that incredible miracle, they shared in the experience of it, and they were blessed because of it.

They saw Jesus and Peter walking together on the water. They watched Jesus and Peter get into the boat. They experienced Jesus coming to their rescue once again when He calmed the storm. Then in awe, they worshipped Him. *What* an experience! *What* a church service!

The disciples were not simply blessed because Peter got out of the boat. They also had the opportunity to be *changed* because he stepped out. Can you imagine the great faith that Peter's miracle must have ignited in their hearts? "Surely," they must have thought, "if Jesus enabled Peter to do the impossible, He would do it for us. If Jesus rescued Peter when he was going down, then He will rescue us. There's no reason to fear stepping out into the unknown with Jesus..."

What an awesome God we serve! By virtue of association, boat people reap the benefits of others!

Christians who've stayed in the boat and missed great opportunities today:

5. You need not fret for there will be other great opportunities tomorrow.

Can you imagine the reaction of the eleven who remained in the boat after it was all said and done? Surely some of them must have regretted that they, too, didn't jump out of the boat and walk on the water with Jesus and Peter. I know I would have.

But thank God, we don't have to live in regret. He's the God of a second chance! The disciples are living proof of the fact that missed opportunities today, don't preclude us from missing out on great opportunities tomorrow. Look at some of the incredible experiences with Jesus that awaited them just around the corner:

- **Mount of Transfiguration:** James and John didn't get out of the boat to walk and on water that night. But they did experience the great transfiguration. (Matthew 17:1-13)

- **Jesus Appearing After His Resurrection:** Thomas really missed it. He was the only one not present the first time Jesus appeared to the disciples after His resurrection. Can you imagine? The last time most of the disciples had seen Jesus was as He died on the cross. How awesome it was for the disciples to experience firsthand that Jesus had truly risen from the grave and was alive forevermore. But Thomas was nowhere to be found that day. When the other eleven tried to convince Thomas that Jesus was alive, he didn't believe them. But eight days later Jesus showed up again, and this time Thomas was there. He touched Jesus' side and saw the nail prints in His hands... (John 20:24-29)

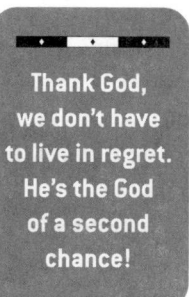

Thank God, we don't have to live in regret. He's the God of a second chance!

- **Pentecost:** The disciples (minus Judas) who missed the opportunity to walk on the water with Jesus all experienced the mighty outpouring of the Holy Spirit on the Day of Pentecost. (Acts 2:1-4)

Although the eleven disciples missed out that stormy night because they chose to be boat people, every single one of them with the exception of Judas, ended up giving everything to Jesus and doing great things in His name. The majority paid the ultimate price for their commitment. Over the years they learned the value and sheer thrill of living their lives *out of the boat.*

Life Outside The Boat

No matter what I'm going through – whether I'm on the mountaintop or in the valley, whether I'm experiencing smooth sailing or stormy waters, I love life. I live with a sense of excitement and expectancy, all the time. Why? Because years ago, I decided that I was *not* going to be a Boat Person. I determined that I was going to follow God's plan for my life. Because of that, He has blessed me beyond words. And, He has taken me places I could have never gone on my own.

The same can be true for you, my friend. No matter where you're at in your journey as a Christian, God has more for you. He's asking, "Will you choose to live outside the boat of mediocrity and casual Christianity? Will you choose My plan for your life instead of yours?"

Say "Yes" to Him! Determine that you're not going to be a boat person; that you're not going to sit back passively on the sidelines of Christianity, watching others do great things for God. Determine that you are going to live outside the boat. Then get ready! He's going to take you places you've never been before!

Questions For Group Discussion

1. In general, what kind of a person am I? One who loves his boat or a water walker?

   _____

   _____

   _____

   _____

   _____

2. Discuss some of the personal tragedies of boat people.

   A. They spend their entire lives watching others experience great moments with God.

   B. They live their lives in paralyzing fear of what might go wrong if they jump out.

   C. They never experience the thrill of having the rescuing hand of God take hold of them.

3. One of the four points of Evan Robert's sermon that ignited the Welsh revival was "Obey the Holy Spirit promptly!" How does this relate to our getting out of the boat when opportunity is placed before us by the LORD?

   _____

   _____

   _____

   _____

   _____

4. What opportunities have you missed personally by staying in the boat?

_____

_____

_____

_____

_____

5. What great moments have you experienced personally in life by stepping out of the boat? What motivated you to step out?

_____

_____

_____

_____

_____

I've Never Been There Before

Lesson 3

THE FACT THAT YOU ARE PARTICIPATING IN THIS STUDY INDICATES THAT you don't want to live life inside the boat. But now what? Get ready, my friend. The Lord wants to take you places you've never been before in Him, and He's going to orchestrate situations and circumstances in your life to help you "get there!"

In this next lesson, we'll gain a deeper understanding about how the Lord will sometimes move in our lives to accomplish His will, and, to *take us where we've never been before.*

A Divine Set-up

I want to preface this lesson by telling you about an experience I once had that left a mark on me forever. It happened years ago in Spain while holding a street crusade. For ten days, we had been faithfully witnessing on the streets with a team of over 100 young people. We had handed out over 25,000 pieces of literature. Our drama team performed several times a day. They were awesome, incredible, yet no one responded to the gospel. Not one single person got saved in ten days!

I had been on a total fast during that whole time. I was going for souls with all my heart. I was going after Spain. I was believing God for a breakthrough in one of the most difficult nations in the world to preach the Gospel.

Jeri and I had always been fruitful in our evangelism. Prior to going to Spain, we had been in the Argentine revival for seven years where hundreds of thousands got saved.

Now in Spain, I was one frustrated person. In all my years of ministry I had never been in a place where we labored so hard but saw absolutely no fruit. It was as if Jesus was on another planet and left me alone in Spain.

Do you think Jesus knew what was going on? Of course He did. He knew everything. He knew what Steve Hill was facing. He could have come down in power the first day. I've seen Him do that before in crusades. But He didn't.

I'm convinced that Jesus *set me up* to take me to a place that I had never been before. Here's what happened. As we were holding a street crusade, the drama team had just performed but the crowd remained absolutely stoic. I was at a loss. Frustrated, I stood before the crowd and did something totally uncharacteristic for me. I dropped the microphone onto the pavement, looked up towards heaven and screamed aloud, **"Jesus, where are You?!"** The crowd was spellbound as this maniac yelled in English to his God.

Then Jesus clearly spoke to me and said, "*I am right over there.*" I looked across the crowd and saw a young man with his hand over his face. I walked through the crowd to him and asked him what was happening. He said, "I don't know, but I feel something. Somebody is touching me." I began to explain what conviction was and what it meant to be touched by Jesus.

I looked around and saw that the whole crowd was listening. At that moment, the Lord said to me, "*Now, now!*" I lifted up my voice and said, "Those of you who want to know Jesus Christ as your Savior, lift your hands." Hands went up all over the crowd. Immediately, the presence of God fell. People began to weep and wail, repenting of their sins and getting saved.

Our team couldn't believe what was happening. Neither could I. For two weeks we had labored ceaselessly with no results. But in an instant, God stepped in and everything changed. I cried my eyes out because I was so scared. I had never experienced anything like this before in my life. *I had entered territory I had never been in before.*

There are times in our lives when God will set us up for an experience to take us where we've never been before. You see, being the creatures of habit that we are, it's so easy to get into a place where we begin to coast in life. We get into a routine. Things are going pretty good. We're in a comfort zone. And before we know it, we begin to stagnate. So the Lord comes along and creates situations to help us grow and go beyond the place where we've settled down.

This brings us to the first point that we need to understand about how the Lord moves in our lives in order to take us where we've never been before.

1. Many times God will purposely set you up for an experience in order to spiritually take you where you've never been before.

This is what happened to me in Spain that day. The Lord orchestrated the circumstances and events to take me someplace I had never been before, and it changed my life.

In lesson two, we learned about the characteristics of Boat People. Now let's pick up where we left off, and focus on Peter who walked on the water. This whole experience was a divine set-up to take Peter and the disciples where they had never gone before.

> *And straightway Jesus constrained his disciples to get into a ship, and to go before him unto the other side, while he sent the multitudes away. And when he had sent the multitudes away, he went up into a mountain apart to pray: and when the evening was come, he was there alone.*
> *(Matthew 14:22-23)*

Did you ever wonder why Jesus constrained, or made, the disciples sail away without Him? Didn't He know that the disciples would encounter a terrible storm where their lives would be in danger? Of course He knew! He knows everything. So *why* did He send the disciples off in that boat without Him? Easy. It was a simple test.

Jesus, Where ARE You?

You've probably asked this question many times, or at least have had it cross your mind. The fact is, there are times in our lives when we go through difficult places and the Lord seems nowhere to be found. We know according to Hebrews 13:5 that He will never leave us nor forsake us. Yet we've all experienced times when the Lord seems to pull away from us and we can't sense His presence. Have you ever wondered why? My friend, if you truly grasp what I'm about to share, it will be a tremendous help to you in your walk with Christ.

At times Jesus pulls away from us:

1. To test our faith

He wants to take you places where you've never been before, and sometimes the only for Him to get you there is by causing you to walk alone for a while and experience something new. The Lord did this with His disciples many times.

Put To The Test With A Lunatic Boy

Remember what took place when Jesus slipped away with Peter, James, and John to the Mount of Transfiguration? The rest of the disciples were left alone and put to the test by an encounter with a demon-possessed boy.

> *And after six days Jesus taketh Peter, James, and John his brother, and bringeth them up into an high mountain apart, And was transfigured before them: and his face did shine as the sun, and his raiment was white as the light...*
>
> *And as they came down from the mountain, Jesus charged them, saying, "Tell the vision to no man, until the Son of man be risen again from the dead." And his disciples asked him, saying, "Why then say the scribes that Elias must first come?" And Jesus answered and said unto them, "Elias truly shall first come, and restore all things. But I say unto you, That Elias is come already, and they knew him not, but have done unto him whatsoever they listed. Likewise shall also the Son of man suffer of them."*
>
> *Then the disciples understood that he spake unto them of John the Baptist. And when they were come to the multitude, there came to him a certain man, kneeling down to him, and saying, "Lord, have mercy on my son: for he is lunatick, and sore vexed: for ofttimes he falleth into the fire, and oft into the water. And I brought him to thy disciples, and they could not cure him."*
> *(Matthew 17:1-2, 9-16)*

Why did Jesus take Peter, James, and John on the Mount of Transfiguration and leave the rest of the disciples down below? He was setting up the rest of the disciples. He knew that at the bottom of the mountain the other disciples were going to be confronted with a demonized, lunatic boy, and that He was going to use the situation to speak to them about their lack of faith.

You know, sometimes we think we are doing so well, and that's about the right time for a rebuke from the Lord! It's in the middle of the storm that we find out what we're made of. It's easy to trust Him when the skies are sunny. It's quite another thing, however, when the storms are raging and it looks like your boat is about to sink.

At times Jesus pulls away from us:

2. To strengthen our walk with Him

I'm convinced that *at other times He pulls away from us to strengthen our walk with Him.* This is a beautiful part of fathering. As parents, we all know that our children grow, mature, and develop skills when we pull away and allow them to experience things on their own.

I remember the first time I let my son Ryan buy something at the store by himself. He was about six years old at the time and had been begging me to buy him a Coke. Finally I said, "There's the concession stand. Go get it yourself." I instructed him on what to do, told him to wait for his change, and then sent him off. The whole time I was watching him.

He came back a few minutes later sipping on the Coke he'd bought by himself. I set my son up to experience something new by withdrawing myself and causing him to step out on his own. The experience strengthened him and helped him to grow.

My son Ryan is now 17 years old. He operates cameras for a major ministry. Those who work with him say that he works like a 21-year old man, and they're amazed at his ability and his hard work. Do you know where Ryan's ability and confidence to do that came from? It came from my pulling from him and allowing him to experience things on his own. These experiences strengthened him and helped him develop confidence.

This reminds me of the story of Martha and Mary at the time when Lazarus died. Did you know that Jesus was only a few miles away when they sent word to Him that Lazarus was dying? Jesus could have walked that distance in less than an hour.

But instead, He waited four days and let Lazarus die before He showed up.

Martha and Mary were heartbroken. Even more, they did not understand why Jesus did not come to them during their hour of crisis. But Jesus did sometime totally unexpected: He raised Lazarus from the dead! Through it all, Martha and Mary came to know Jesus in a way they had not known Him before, and their faith and confidence in Him skyrocketed as they learned to trust Him even in the midst of circumstances they didn't understand.

At times Jesus pulls away from us:

3. To lead us into territory we've never been before

There are also times when Jesus will pull away from us to cause us to do things that we've never done before. This is what happened to the disciples that night on the stormy sea. Let me ask you a question. Did Jesus know that the wind was going to blow, and the ship was going to be tossed? Did He know that disciples would fear for their lives? Of course. He knows everything. So why did He send the disciples off into the storm without Him? Because He wanted them to go through things they'd never gone through before!

In each of these situations – when the disciples saw Jesus walk on the water, when they encountered a demon they couldn't cast out, and when Mary and Martha witnessed Jesus raise Lazarus from the dead, the Lord led the disciples into places they had never been before.

Remember this the next time you go through a time when the Lord seems distant. It could be that He is taking you someplace you've never been before.

> At times He pulls away from us to strengthen our walk with Him. This is a beautiful part of fathering.

2. Many times Jesus will appear on the scene at the darkest point of your trial in order to take you where you've never been before.

Think about some of the deep, dark places you've gone through in life. In the midst of that situation, it may have seemed like Jesus was nowhere to be found. But then, at your darkest hour when you were at a loss for what to do, Jesus stepped on the scene and brought you through.

The natural tendency would be to sit back and wonder why the Lord would wait until you're at your darkest point before bringing the answer. The disciples probably wondered the same thing that night on the stormy sea.

They had been rowing all night. It was now the fourth watch, somewhere between 3:00am to 6:00am. That's the darkest part of the night. They were exhausted. Their strength was gone. Their lives were in danger. All hope seemed gone. It was at this point that Jesus showed up.

> *But now the ship was now in the midst of the sea, tossed with waves: for the wind was contrary. And in the fourth watch of the night Jesus went unto them, walking on the sea.* *(Matthew 14:24-25)*

From the Mountain to the Valley

There's an important lesson here that the Lord wants us to understand. Look at what happened just *before* and immediately *after* the storm. Before the storm, the disciples experienced the awesome miracle with Jesus of the feeding of the five thousand (Matthew 14:13-21). Immediately after the storm, they saw Jesus perform awesome miracles and heal every single person at Gennesaret (Matthew 14:34-36).

> "The devil is always waiting at the foot of the mountain."
> - D.L. Moody

Sandwiched between two great mountain top experiences was the wind and the storm. And so it is with our lives. You can go from a sunny day to a threatening storm in a matter of hours. And like this story, a deep trial often follows a great victory.

My friend, the Christian life is a constant journey filled with incredible highs and unwelcome lows. Have you ever had a deep trial right after a great victory? D.L. Moody said it best when he said, "The devil is always waiting at the foot of the mountain."

Jesus knows what you're going through. It could be the fourth watch of your sickness and the doctors say, "It's over!" That's the deepest, darkest part of the night, and that's usually when we get serious. Or perhaps you've lost your job, or your kids are in trouble. Did you know that He is always interceding and praying for you? When you are exhausted, He's strong. The same water that you're sinking in, He's walking upon!

Some of the greatest experiences I've had in God were at the deepest, darkest parts of my life. We all go through stuff. What's going on in your life? Are you passing through an extremely difficult time? Start looking for Jesus walking on the water, and get ready. The Lord is about to take you where you've never been before.

3. Often God will prod you to do the impossible in order to take you where you've never been before.

Let's look again at the story of the disciples on the raging sea. They had rowed all night. They were exhausted. Their boat was full of water. Suddenly Jesus appeared on the scene, walking on the water. Now here's where it gets interesting.

> And when the disciples saw him walking on the sea, they were troubled, saying, "It is a spirit; and they cried out for fear." But straightway Jesus spake unto them, saying, "Be of good cheer; it is I;

The same water that you're sinking in, He's walking upon.

be not afraid." And Peter answered him and said, "Lord, if it be thou, bid me come unto thee on the water." And he said, "Come." And when Peter was come down out of the ship, he walked on the water, to go to Jesus. (Matthew 14:26-29)

Everyone knows you can't walk on water. It's impossible. The disciples knew it. Peter knew it. But Jesus set Peter up to do the impossible.

He'll do the same with you. He'll prod you to do the impossible. Why? To take you places you've never been before. Perhaps your cancer-ridden neighbor looks at you and asks, "Do you think God can heal me?" *You've never prayed for someone like this before.* And all the while, God is nudging you to step out and pray for your neighbor to be healed.

Or perhaps the Lord prods you one day to witness to a stranger. You see someone sitting on a chair and God speaks to your heart and says, "Go talk to that man about Jesus." And, because you stepped out of your comfort zone and obeyed the Lord, suddenly life is different for you. Why? Because when God prodded you, you stepped out and allowed Him to take you where you've never been before.

I remember an encounter I had once with a demon-possessed girl. I was scared to death to pray for her because she looked like a witch. She was dressed in black and she kept staring at me with this evil, glassy look in her eyes. She was scary. She spoke Spanish and I only spoke English at the time. I looked all around for my interpreter, but he had disappeared, so I had to deal with the situation by myself. Once again, the Lord set me up to take me someplace I had never been before.

The Lord said to me, "Say My name." I said to the Lord, "But Jesus, I don't even know how to say Your name in Spanish..." He said again, "Say My name, Steve." I looked into her eyes and I said aloud, "Jesus!" She instantly fell to the ground and began wreathing and vomiting. Her body was moving in all sorts of contortions. I quickly knelt beside her and repeatedly spoke His name saying, "Jesus. Jesus. Jesus. Jesus. Jesus..." I learned something that day, my friend. So often we want to counsel people out of every situation, when God simply wants to come down in power. Just speaking the name of Jesus that day caused those demons to flee.

4. The majority of Christians are content with looking at Jesus from the security of their own boat because they don't want to go where they have never been before.

A fair weather Christian is someone who can be counted on when there are signs and wonders, or when things are easy and the sun is shining. Who wouldn't want to follow Jesus for the fishes and loaves? But when a storm comes along and rocks their boats, they bail-out.

Many want to walk on water, but they don't want to be in the boat in a storm. You've got to be *in* the boat during the storm in order to experience walking on water. Others get *within sight* of God, but never get a thing *from* Him. We could learn a lesson from the two thieves on the cross. Both were the same distance from the Lord. One got saved while the other died and went to hell.

I've seen it over and over again in our services throughout the years. Two people are in the same church service. One hears the Word, responds to the Lord and is changed, while the other thinks that the message was for everyone else and he remains unchanged.

If we could hear from the woman with issue of blood who pressed through the crowd to touch the hem of His garment, blind Bartimaeus who made a nuisance of himself by crying out to Jesus, or Zacchaeus who climbed a tree to get to Jesus, each of them would tell us about how they stepped out of their boats of comfort and did whatever it took to get to Jesus. As a result, each one of them received a miracle from the Lord.

If they were here today, they'd encourage us to press past our insecurities, fears, circumstances and what other people say, and step out of the boat to lay hold of what God has for us in life.

Many people want to experience great things from God, but they don't want the great trials that come with it. But it comes with the territory. You can't have one without the other. Jesus told us this when He said that those who follow Him would be blessed, but that they'd also suffer persecution in this life.

> *So Jesus answered and said, "Assuredly, I say to you, there is no one who has left house or brothers or sisters or father or mother or wife or children or lands, for My sake and the gospel's, who shall not receive a hundredfold now in this time–houses and brothers and sisters and mothers and children and lands, with persecutions–and in the age to come, eternal life..."* (Mark 10:29-30, NKJV)

The Paradox

Think about this. Those who remained in the boat that night really weren't safe and secure at all. They were in desperate circumstances beyond their control. They were drenched. Their boat was filling up with water, and their lives were in danger. The paradox of the whole situation is the fact that the safest place to be that night was out on the stormy waters *with* Jesus, rather than in the sinking boat *without* Him.

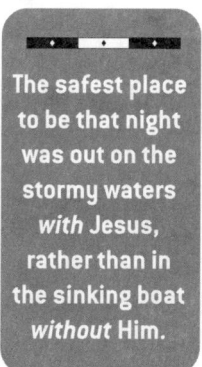

The safest place to be that night was out on the stormy waters *with* Jesus, rather than in the sinking boat *without* Him.

That reminds me of something I once heard a minister say concerning missions work. He'd say, "You're safer on the foreign mission field *in* the will of God, than you are in America *out* of the will of God."

My friend, Jesus is your only refuge and true place of safety. I'd rather be walking with Him in the midst of stormy seas, than staying in a sinking boat without Him, any day. Determine that you're going to stay close to

Him, and that wherever He leads, you're going to follow. There, with Him, will you find your refuge and security.

5. *When you begin to falter by doing what is natural, put your faith in Jesus who lives in the supernatural and He will take you where you have never been before.*

I've got good news for you, my friend. When, not if, you begin to falter by doing what is *natural,* put your faith in Jesus who lives in the *supernatural,* and He will take you where you've never been before!

The *natural* thing for Peter when he stepped out of the boat was to falter and sink. After all, nobody can walk on water! Peter knew that, but he stepped out anyway. And when he began to do what was natural (i.e., sink), Jesus, who lives in the supernatural, lifted him up and enabled him to do what was unnatural and humanly impossible. He enabled him to walk on the water.

Some Things You Just Can't Practice

Have you ever thought about it? You can't practice walking on water, working a miracle, or doing great things for God, any more than you can practice getting saved. You have to experience these places in God. And each time you step out into uncharted territory with Jesus, He's going to lead you into something fresh – a brand new place with Him.

That's what happened to me in Spain when I cried out in desperation, "*Jesus, where are You?*" And He answered, "I'm right over here, Steve." There's no way I could have practiced what was about to happen next. It took a ten-day fast. It took laboring on the streets. It took talking to thousand's of people

> You can't practice walking on water, working a miracle, or doing great things for God. You have to experience these places in God.

about the Lord, getting blank stares, cursings and absolute rejection. I was just like the disciples out on the stormy sea. I had exhausted my strength. My boat was being tossed. Jesus was nowhere in sight. But as I cried out to Him in desperation, all of a sudden He showed up on the scene and said, "Steve...I'm right over here. I want you to go somewhere you've never been before. You've labored and toiled and exhausted your strength with no results. Now come here, son, and watch how I can touch just one man and turn this whole crowd to Me." And He did!

Dealing With Doubts

Here's something important to remember. It's perfectly natural to have doubts. But Peter leaves us with the divine methodology of dealing with our doubts and fears. He didn't say, "Lord, bid me to walk on the water," focusing on the natural elements of the water, the waves and his own inability. Instead he said, "Jesus, bid me to come to *You*." My friend, when you step out to follow Jesus, He will take you where you've never been before.

Some get hung up on Peter sinking. But that's the most irrelevant part of the whole story. Whenever I read the story of Peter walking on the water, I never see him sinking. I'm always blown away by the fact that he got out of the boat. Period.

The Whole Picture

When you go through a struggle, the important thing is to get back up!

My friend, God is not looking at your sinking. He's looking at your reaching out to Him. This is why you must learn to look at the whole picture of your life rather than your little stumblings. Quit beating yourself up because you fall. When you go through a struggle, the important thing is to get back up!

Remember, this same Peter who walked on the water was also the disciple who had the revelation that Christ was the Son of the Living God. But soon after, he cursed and denied that he even knew the Lord. Then, days later, Jesus picked him to preach that great message on the day of Pentecost.

When we look at a cross section of Peter's life – the ups and downs, the signs and wonders, the depth of his falling and his struggles – when we think of the patriarchs and the great men of faith, Peter is always one of those at the top of our list. We think of him as a man of God.

Heaven loves people who rise up in faith, step out of their comfort zones and say, "Jesus, take me somewhere I have never been before" and then, like Peter, they step out of the boat.

Questions for Group Discussion

1. Do you feel that the LORD has ever purposely "set you up" that He might spiritually take you where you've never been before? Explain.

   _____

   _____

   _____

2. There are times when Jesus seems to pull away from us and is nowhere to be found. Discuss the following reasons why the Lord might pull away from us:

   A. To test our faith.

   _____

   _____

   _____

   B. To strengthen our walk with Him.

   _____

   _____

   _____

   C. To lead us into territory we've never been before.

   _____

   _____

   _____

3. Discuss a trial you went through where Jesus appeared on the scene, walking on the water at your darkest hour. How did this change your life and walk with Him?

_____

_____

_____

4. Has Jesus ever prodded you to do the impossible? _____ How did you react?

_____

_____

_____

Why does He prod us to do these things?

_____

_____

_____

5. How does our daily walk in the natural affect our participation in the supernatural?

_____

_____

_____

God's Risky Radicals

STEPPING OUT OF THE BOAT AND VENTURING WHERE YOU'VE NEVER gone before requires taking risk and being radical.

The Lord is looking for those who will expose themselves to risk and be radical for Him.

What's A Risky Radical?

To go places you've never gone before in God requires **risk**. The word *"risk"* means *"to expose yourself to uncertain hazard or danger."* This could be any type of hazard or danger, not just physical.

Going places you've never gone before and doing new things also requires being **radical**. *"A radical"* is *"one who advocates extreme measures,"* or *"a person who overturns or changes the present state of things."*

A **Risky Radical** is someone who is willing to expose himself to uncertain hazard or danger in order to make a change in his world. I've been accused of being a radical my whole Christian life.

Throughout the Bible, we find those who were willing to become *Risky Radicals* for God. These men and women put their all on

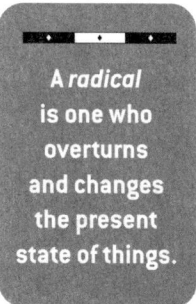

A *radical* is one who overturns and changes the present state of things.

the line for Him. As a result, God used them to do the impossible, and at times, to change the circumstances of their day.

Elijah: The Radical Who Boldly Confronted Sin & Idolatry

Elijah ("Jehovah is my God") risked his life when he confronted the idolatrous prophets of Baal. Of all the prophets, he was by far the most outstanding. Jehovah sent him to eradicate the worship of Baal during the reign of King Ahab of the Northern Kingdom of Israel. He appeared on the world scene with incredible courage and a tremendous zeal for God. Elijah boldly stood before the magnificent court of King Ahab in his humble prophet's attire and declared in the name of the Lord that there would be no dew or rain in the land except at his word (I Kings 17:1).

We all know the risk that he took as he radically confronted the false prophets of Baal on Mt. Carmel, causing the people to forsake their worship of Baal and return to the LORD.

> *And Elijah said unto the prophets of Baal, "Choose you one bullock for yourselves, and dress it first; for ye are many; and call on the name of your gods, but put no fire under." And they took the bullock which was given them, and they dressed it, and called on the name of Baal from morning even until noon, saying, "O Baal, hear us." But there was no voice, nor any that answered. And they leaped upon the altar which was made.*
>
> *And it came to pass at noon, that Elijah mocked them, and said, "Cry aloud: for he is a god; either he is talking, or he is pursuing, or he is in a journey, or peradventure he sleepeth, and must be awaked." And they cried aloud, and cut themselves after their manner with knives and*

lancets, till the blood gushed out upon them. And it came to pass, when midday was past, and they prophesied until the time of the offering of the evening sacrifice, that there was neither voice, nor any to answer, nor any that regarded.

And Elijah said unto all the people, "Come near unto me." And all the people came near unto him. And he repaired the altar of the LORD that was broken down. And Elijah took twelve stones, according to the number of the tribes of the sons of Jacob, unto whom the word of the LORD came, saying, "Israel shall be thy name:" And with the stones he built an altar in the name of the LORD: and he made a trench about the altar, as great as would contain two measures of seed. And he put the wood in order, and cut the bullock in pieces, and laid him on the wood, and said, "Fill four barrels with water, and pour it on the burnt sacrifice, and on the wood."

And he said, "Do it the second time." And they did it the second time.

And he said, "Do it the third time." And they did it the third time. And the water ran round about the altar; and he filled the trench also with water.

And it came to pass at the time of the offering of the evening sacrifice, that Elijah the prophet came near, and said, "LORD God of Abraham, Isaac, and of Israel, let it be known this day that thou art God in Israel, and that I am thy servant, and that I have done all these things at thy word. Hear me, O LORD, hear me, that this people may know that thou art the LORD God, and that thou hast turned their heart back again."

Then the fire of the LORD fell, and consumed the burnt sacrifice, and the wood, and the stones, and the dust, and licked up the water that was in

the trench. And when all the people saw it, they
fell on their faces: and they said, "The LORD, he
is the God; the LORD, he is the God."

And Elijah said unto them, "Take the
prophets of Baal; let not one of them escape."
And they took them: and Elijah brought them
down to the brook Kishon, and slew them there.
(I Kings 18:25-40)

Elijah was the evangelist of his day. His voice thundered
with clear warnings to those entrapped in idolatry as he faced the
false prophets of Baal. Knowing that he could lose his head, he
boldly confronted their sin, which resulted in one of the greatest
stories in church history - Elijah calling down fire on Mt. Carmel
and then executing the 450 prophets of Baal. No doubt about it,
Elijah was definitely one of God's Risky Radicals!

The Queen Who Risked Her Life

Another Risky Radical was an extraordinary woman of
God named Esther who lived 500 years before Christ. She was
an orphan Jewish captive who was elevated to the throne as
Queen of Persia. During her reign as queen, a wicked man named
Haaman connived a plot to exterminate the Jews.

We're all familiar with Mordecai's timely, prophetic words
to Esther when he said,

"For if thou altogether holdest thy peace at this
time, then shall there enlargement and deliverance
arise to the Jews from another place; but thou and
thy father's house shall be destroyed: and who
knoweth whether thou art come to the kingdom
for such a time as this?" *(Esther 4:14)*

Esther secured a remarkable deliverance for the Jews by
stepping in and placing her own life on the line in order to do

something great for God. She was a powerful woman of God, and definitely one of God's Risky Radicals.

John the Baptist

In Matthew 14, we find the account of John the Baptist who risked his life as he fearlessly confronted both Herod and the religious people of his day.

> *Now Herod had arrested John and bound him and put him in prison because of Herodias, his brother Philip's wife, for John had been saying to him: "It is not lawful for you to have her." Herod wanted to kill John, but he was afraid of the people, because they considered him a prophet.   (Matthew 14:3-5)*

John was faithful to do what God had called him to do to the point of death. When he denounced Herod for the sin of adultery, it cost him his life. Look at Jesus' testimony of John:

> *"I tell you the truth: Among those born of women there has not risen anyone greater than John the Baptist; yet he who is least in the kingdom of heaven is greater than he. From the days of John the Baptist until now, the kingdom of heaven has been forcefully advancing, and forceful men lay hold of it."   (Matthew 11:11-12)*

Every Move Of God Has Risky Radicals At The Forefront

If space permitted, we could speak of other radicals such as David who fearlessly slew Goliath with just a slingshot and a

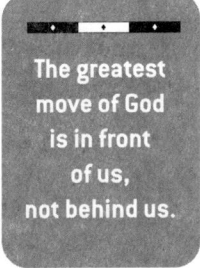

The greatest move of God is in front of us, not behind us.

few small stones, of Jonah who confronted the people of Nineveh, of Peter who walked on the water, or of Stephen who put his life on the line as he preached to the religious leaders.

Over the years, I've studied church history, including the great revivals of the past. I've also been involved in two major revivals. Here's what I've found: every historical move of God has had Risky Radicals at the forefront.

I'm convinced that the greatest move of God the world has ever seen is in front of us, not behind us. That being the case, it is the responsibility of every one of us to take seriously the call of God that is upon our generation and upon our individual lives to make a difference in our world. We must prepare ourselves individually and corporately for this mighty move of God.

Perhaps you've heard it said before, *"if you keep doing what you're doing, you're going to keep getting what you've been getting."* Spiritually speaking, there's truth in this statement. The opposite is also true. If I choose to go to higher heights and deeper depths with the Lord, if I choose to believe Him for greater things, then according to my faith so be it.

In 2 Chronicles 16:9 we are told that "the eyes of the LORD range throughout the earth..." He's looking for those He can mightily use in the coming days. But just what is He looking for?

God is scanning the earth in search of believers:

1. Who are willing to change their ROUTINE in order to make a difference in this world.

A *routine* is a regular procedure. It's what's customary or prescribed. Every one of us has a routine. I automatically wake up at 5:00 a.m. every morning. Then I have a cup of coffee and immediately go into prayer. After I spend time in prayer, I go out and exercise. Every morning I have this routine. It's like clockwork to me. I don't have to think about it.

While routines are good and necessary, sometimes they can actually hinder you from moving into what God has for you. That's why you must be willing to change your routine if you're going to do anything for God.

Have you ever thought about what might have happened if some men and women of God had not been willing to change their routines? Consider the following:

If **David** had not been willing to change his routine of tending sheep to answering the call of God to slay Goliath, he would never have been promoted and eventually become king. He had to change his routine.

If **Noah** had not been willing to change his routine to begin constructing the ark, who knows what would have happened!

If **Jonah** had not repented and been willing to change his routine after soaking in the gastric juices of that big fish, he would never have succeeded in winning the Ninevites.

If **the woman with the issue of blood** had not been willing to change her routine and use the last bit of her energy to touch the hem of Jesus' garment, she would never have been healed.

If **the blind man** in John 9 had not been willing to change his routine and follow the instructions of Jesus to wash in the pool of Siloam, he would have never been healed.

If **Peter** had not been willing to change his routine of fishing to follow Jesus, he would never have become a fisher of men. If he had not been willing to change his routine and wait in the upper room, he would not have been baptized in the Holy Spirit and used mightily in preaching repentance.

If **Martin Luther** had not been willing to change from his legalistic, traditional routine of worship to an intimate relationship with God, there would not have been a Reformation.

If **John Wesley** and **George Whitfield** had not been willing to change their routine from preaching in churches to preaching in

> If you're going to do anything for God, you must be willing to change your routine.

A *Risky Radical* is someone who RELIES on God to do what they can't do in their own strength or ability.

the open-air, there would not have been the greatest revival in English history.

If **William Seymour** had not been willing to change his routine and move from the porch of that small house to a larger facility, there would not have been an Azusa Street Revival.

I thank God that William Seymour was a risk-taker. You may remember that the Azusa Street Revival started inside a small house on Bonnie Brey Street. They quickly outgrew the house and spilled out to the front porch. When the front porch became too small, William Seymour took a risk by deciding to change locations. It was risky because any time God is moving, the tendency is to question whether or not His presence will move with you if you change something. Thank God, William Seymour took a risk and changed the routine.

What changes may the Lord be requiring of you? Some may be temporary, while others may be lifestyle changes. Perhaps He's speaking to your heart to free up your schedule so you can get involved in your church Easter drama. Or maybe He's leading you to a special time of prayer and fasting to obtain an answer to prayer. Or maybe He's prompting you to use your bonus check to go on a mission's trip instead of vacationing in the Caribbean. Or He may be dealing with you about rising up an hour earlier every day so that you have the quality time you need to seek His face.

If you ask Him, He'll show you where you need to make changes in your routine to be one of His *Risky Radicals*.

God is scanning the earth in search of believers:

2. Who have learned how to RELY on Him in order to make a difference in this world.

"To rely" means to trust or to depend on someone. A Risky Radical – someone who's going to do something for God – is

someone who RELIES on God to do what they can't do in their own strength or ability. We all remember when David stood before the giant Goliath in I Samuel 17. As he faced Goliath he boldly declared,

> *"...You come to me with a sword, with a spear, and with a javelin. But I come to you in the name of the LORD of hosts, the God of the armies of Israel, whom you have defied. This day the LORD will deliver you into my hand, and I will strike you and take your head from you. And this day I will give the carcasses of the camp of the Philistines to the birds of the air and the wild beasts of the earth, that all the earth may know that there is a God in Israel. Then all this assembly shall know that the LORD does not save with sword and spear; for the battle is the LORD's, and He will give you into our hands."*
> *(I Samuel 17:45b-47)*

I love how David declared that his victory over Goliath would cause Israel to know that *"the Lord does not save with sword and spear; for the battle is the Lord's."* Evidently Israel was depending upon the sword and the spear to win their victory. Consequently, they were defeated before ever going into battle. David on the other hand, was not relying upon Saul's armor or upon his skill in swinging a slingshot. Nor was he looking at his inabilities or the giant that stood before him. He was relying upon God. Period.

There's a lesson in here for us to learn. The human tendency is to focus on either your abilities or your inabilities. But either one will set you up for defeat. *If you're going to be someone who God can use to bring about change, you must learn how to rely on God!*

Remember the three radical young men, Shadrach, Meshach, and Abed-nego, who were thrown into the fire for refusing to bow down and worship the golden image of King Nebuchadnezzar (Daniel 3:14-26)? Talk about risk! They knew that their refusal to bow down and worship the image would probably cost them their lives, yet they risked their lives to take a stand for their God. As a result, they walked through the fiery furnace with the fourth man! Everybody wants to experience the fourth man, but nobody wants the fire! Are you willing to take that kind of risk for God?

Relying on God to Reach the Lost

Let me bring this down home to where we live. There are people you know who need Jesus. It may be that you don't witness to them because you can't stand the way people treat you. They say things like, "Get out of here with your Christianity. Who do you think you are, holier than thou?!" Usually when they say that I respond with, "That's a good point! Perhaps I am holier than you. I've given up my bad habits; I live for God; I keep my thought life clean. There's a good chance that I am holier than thou." That really gets them upset!

My suggestion is that when you're witnessing to somebody and they get mad, you might as well just go for it. They can't stand your Christian lifestyle anyhow, so you might as well go ahead and preach to them. But always remember this: they're not upset at you. If you spoke about motorcycles (Harley Davidson's, of course), fishing, cooking, or the latest reality television show, they'd talk all day with you. It's because you bring up that five-letter name, "Jesus," that they turn on you. They're not at war with you – it's Jesus they have the problem with.

> Everybody wants to experience the fourth man, but nobody wants the fire!

The Bible says they spoke evil of Jesus, and they're going to speak evil of you. They got mad at Him, and they're going to get mad at you. They persecuted the Lord; they're going to persecute you. But a Risky Radical learns how to rely on and draw strength from the Lord in the midst of such opposition.

88

The Power of Tears

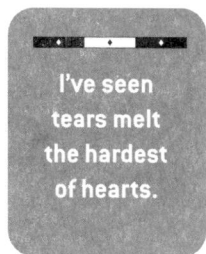

I've seen tears melt the hardest of hearts.

There's truth to the old saying, "People don't want to know how much you know until they know how much you care." There have been times when I hit a brick wall while trying to get someone saved. On many occasions, tears would begin to stream down my face as I told them how I cared for their soul. My friend, I've seen those tears melt the hardest of hearts, time and time again.

One other word of wisdom regarding witnessing. Make sure that your walk measures up to your talk. In other words, make sure that people can see Jesus in how you live your life – that what you *do* measures up to what you *say*.

God is scanning the earth in search of believers:

3. Who are not afraid of causing a RIOT in order to make a difference in this world.

"*Riot*" means a turbulent disturbance; confusion; to move or act with wild abandonment.

When we think of the word "riot," most of us think of an absolutely chaotic event. But that is an extreme riot. A riot is any type of turbulent disturbance. To put it simply, when you become one of God's *Risky Radicals,* you stir the waters around you!

Look at the uproar that Paul and Silas caused as they preached the Gospel in Thessalonica. Many came to believe on Christ and as a result, a group of envious, unbelieving Jews stirred up trouble and assaulted the house of Jason looking for Paul and Silas.

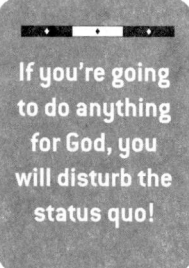

If you're going to do anything for God, you will disturb the status quo!

And some of them were persuaded; and a great multitude of the devout Greeks, and not a few of the leading women, joined Paul and Silas. But the Jews who were not persuaded, becoming envious, took some of the evil men from the marketplace, and gathering a mob, set all the city in an uproar and attacked the house of Jason, and sought to bring them out to the people. But when they did not find them, they dragged Jason and some brethren to the rulers of the city, crying out, "These who have turned the world upside down have come here too. Jason has harbored them, and these are all acting contrary to the decrees of Caesar, saying there is another king–Jesus." (Acts 17:4-7, NKJV)

Paul and Silas caused such a disturbance preaching the Gospel that they were accused of "turning the world upside down!" That's one accusation I'd like to have laid up to my charge! How about you?!

Disturbing the Status Quo

If you're going to do anything for God, you *will* disturb the status quo! You can disturb the status quo in your home by involving yourself in the church Christmas production. The time and effort that you invest going to practices, learning your part, and helping to design the set will disturb the normal routine of you and your family. But without everyone making the required dedication and commitment to step out of the norm and cause a disturbance by changing their routine, there wouldn't be a Christmas drama with souls getting saved.

Awhile back a man got a hold of a video of my message, *When The Gavel Falls*, which is all about the judgment of God. He was trying to get his lost loved ones saved. While visiting at his wife's brother's house, he got up early one morning, put the video on and turned up the volume really loud so his family could hear it. The family came in. His wife's brother's girlfriend also came in and sat down. She was riveted to the message. After watching the video, she got up and left the room. Ten minutes later she came back screaming that she was going to hell if she didn't get saved. She gave her life to Jesus Christ and is now on fire for God and going to church. In fact, she's taking her family to church. But her boyfriend is fuming mad at what has happened.

This man caused a riot or a disturbance in his family! The girlfriend also caused a riot (a turbulent disturbance) in her relationship with her boyfriend.

Young person, when you raise your voice and start talking about Jesus at school, things may not go so smoothly. You're disturbing the status quo.

Sir, when you take a stand at work to honor the Lord in all of your business dealings, some people might get mad at you. And when you refuse to listen to dirty jokes, you may ruffle a few feathers.

Mom and Dad, when you determine that it's more important for your kids to be in church than it is for them to participate in their favorite Sunday sport, you may cause a riot or a disturbance in your home. But you and your children will be blessed for honoring the Lord and putting Him first.

My friend, these kinds of riots are wonderful because they are centered around what God is doing!

God is scanning the earth in search of believers:

4. Who would like to receive a REWARD for making a difference in this world.

A reward is something you receive in return for the work that you've rendered. An Oscar or a Golden Globe is awarded to actors for an incredible performance, the Gold Medal to the best Olympic athletes, the Heisman Trophy to the most outstanding college football player, and the Pulitzer

> God always calls us to do something that we can't do ourselves. If we could do it ourselves, then it's not faith.

Prize to those who distinguish themselves in journalism and fine arts. The prestigious Nobel Prize is awarded to those who make significant contributions to society in the areas of science, medicine, literature, peace or economics.

These rewards are earned by the best of the best for a lifetime of hard work and exceptional accomplishments. And only a handful of people will ever receive such an honorable award for their life's work. But as distinguished and prestigious as these rewards may be, they are temporal, and the glory and honor that they bring will one day fade away. But there is a reward that's eternal, and God is searching the earth for believers who want to receive His reward.

Living for Eternity

When Jeri and I came off the mission field, we moved our ministry base to Lindale, Texas, where I had the privilege of being mentored by Leonard Ravenhill for three years. Leonard was a tremendous man of God who was more at home in the prayer closet than anywhere else. In his later years, preachers would come from around the world just to spend a few hours with him and glean from his wisdom, his life experience, and his walk with God.

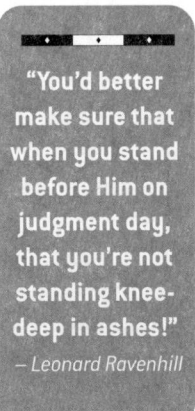

"You'd better make sure that when you stand before Him on judgment day, that you're not standing knee-deep in ashes!"

– Leonard Ravenhill

One very early morning, Leonard called me up and said, "Steve, I want you to make me a sign." He knew that I enjoyed graphic arts and sign painting. "Sure, Leonard," I replied, "I'd be glad to. What do you want the sign to say?" "Eternity." "Eternity?" "Yes." "Anything else?" "No. Just the word *eternity*." "Okay."

So I made the sign and brought it over to his house later that day. When I asked him where he wanted the sign, he replied, "Put it on the ceiling." "On the ceiling?" "Yes, because every time I look up and see that sign, I will be reminded of eternity…"

Leonard lived for eternity. He went home to be with the Lord in 1994. Now, he's on the other side of eternity. He's received his reward for living for God while on the earth. If he were here today, he'd tell you to listen to what I'm saying and to live for eternity every day of your life.

Something else Leonard used to say to me was, "Steve, you'd better make sure that when you stand before Him on the judgment day, that you're not standing knee-deep in ashes!"

This is exactly what Paul was telling us when he said to the church at Corinth:

> *According to the grace of God which is given unto me, as a wise masterbuilder, I have laid the foundation, and another buildeth thereon.* **But let every man take heed how he buildeth thereupon.** *For other foundation can no man lay than that is laid, which is Jesus Christ. Now if any man build upon this foundation gold, silver, precious stones, wood, hay, stubble; Every man's work shall be made manifest: for the day shall declare it, because it shall be revealed by fire;* **and the fire shall try every man's work of what sort it is. If any man's work abide which he hath built thereupon, he shall receive a reward.** *If any man's work shall be burned, he shall suffer loss: but he himself shall be saved; yet so as by fire.*   (I Corinthians 3:10-15)

Would to God that every Christian took this scripture seriously! How it would transform our lives, not to mention our eternal reward!

Heaven Knows!

I've always been fascinated by the fact that heaven keeps record of what we do and how we live our lives on earth! Look at these scriptures that link our works on earth to our eternal reward in heaven:

> *And I saw the dead, small and great, stand before God; and the books were opened: and another book was opened, which is the book of life: and the dead were judged out of those things which were written in the books, according to their works.*
> *(Revelation 20:12)*

> *For the Son of man shall come in the glory of his Father with his angels; and then he shall reward every man according to his works. (Matthew 16:27)*

Heaven, my friend, keeps track of:

> Every time you've ever witnessed to someone.
> Every soul that you've ever led to Jesus.
> Every time you've reached out to bless someone.
> Every prayer you've ever prayed on behalf of others.
> Every word of encouragement that you've ever spoken.
> Every dollar you've ever sowed into the Kingdom.
> Every sacrifice you've ever made for the cause of Christ.
> Every act of obedience.
> Every step of faith.
> Every thing that you've ever said, given, or done to bless His name.

As the years go by, you may forget many of the works that you've done in His name, but *Jesus never forgets!* Look at what Hebrews tells us:

> *For God is not unrighteous to forget your work and labour of love, which ye have shewed toward his name, in that ye have ministered to the saints, and do minister. And we desire that every one of you do shew the same diligence to the full assurance of hope*

unto the end: That ye be not slothful, but followers of them who through faith and patience inherit the promises. *(Hebrews 6:10-12)*

His Reward

The Lord will not forget your work and your labor of love! My friend, the Lord *wants* you to inherit His promises! That's why you must be diligent unto the end – so you can receive His reward! The Bible gives us a glimpse of what awaits us:

For those who forsake all to follow Him

And everyone that hath forsaken houses, or brethren, or sisters, or father, or mother, or wife, or children, or lands, for my name's sake, shall receive an hundredfold, and shall inherit everlasting life. *(Matthew 19:29)*

For those who are faithful and finish their race

For I am already being poured out like a drink offering, and the time has come for my departure. I have fought the good fight, I have finished the race, I have kept the faith. Now there is in store for me the crown of righteousness, which the Lord, the righteous Judge, will award to me on that day-and not only to me, but also to all who have longed for his appearing. *(2 Timothy 4:6-8, NIV)*

Stephen caught a glimpse of his reward

But he, being full of the Holy Ghost, looked up stedfastly into heaven, and saw the glory of God, and Jesus standing on the right hand of God, And

*said, Behold, I see the heavens opened, and the
Son of man standing on the right hand of God.
(Acts 7:55-56)*

Run the Race

In Hebrews 11, the great "Hall of Faith," we find those who
were rewarded *up there* in heaven for being Risky Radicals while
down here on the earth.

*These all died in faith, not having received the
promises, but having seen them afar off, and
were persuaded of them, and embraced them, and
confessed that they were strangers and pilgrims
on the earth. For they that say such things declare
plainly that they seek a country. And truly, if they
had been mindful of that country from whence
they came out, they might have had opportunity
to have returned. But now they desire a better
country, that is, an heavenly: wherefore* **God is
not ashamed to be called their God: for he hath
prepared for them a city.** *(Hebrews 11:13-16)*

Most of us have family up in heaven, myself included. Just
two weeks after we started Heartland Fellowship, my mother
suddenly died. She's up in heaven now and she's got a reward for
praying me into the kingdom...and for everything else she did
here on earth for God.

The Lord is SEARCHING the earth for believers who want
to receive His reward! God has rewards laid up for all who will
"go for the gold." He's looking for those who are willing to take
a risk, step outside of themselves, and live their lives for eternity.
This is why we're instructed to *lay aside every weight, and the
sin which doth so easily beset us, and let us run with patience the
race that is set before us* (Hebrews 12:1).

Answer The Call

The reason why many people and churches never move forward is because they want to stay in their comfort zone. But God always calls us to do something that we can't do ourselves. If we could do it ourselves, then it's not faith.

God is looking for those who are willing to take a risk, step out in faith and believe Him to do the impossible. When He finds such a person or a group of people, He looks and says, "Finally, someone who is willing to take a risk. Someone who is willing to believe Me for the impossible." Or, "Finally, there's a people, a church, that's serious about what's important to Me. They're interested in My kingdom. They love souls. They seek My face. They welcome My presence and My power. They live holy. They believe My Word…"

Are you willing to break out of your **ROUTINE**, to **RELY** on Him to do what you can't do yourself, and to cause a disturbance or **RIOT** as you step out in faith to do something for God?

If you answer the call to be one of God's Risky Radicals, then on that day when you stand before Him, you will receive a **REWARD** for making a difference in this world. And that, my friend, is a reward worth living for!

Questions for Group Discussion

1. What does it mean to be a Risky Radical for the LORD? Discuss.

   _____

   _____

   _____

   _____

2. Discuss the life and ministry of three of the LORD'S Risky Radicals: Elijah, Queen Esther, and John the Baptist.

   _____

   _____

   _____

   _____

3. "The eyes of the LORD range throughout the earth" looking for Risky Radicals among His people! Discuss the qualifications associated with Risky Radicals that He is in search of today. Believers who:

   • Are willing to change their ROUTINE in order to make a difference in this world.

   _____

   _____

   _____

- Have learned to RELY on Him in order to make a difference in this world.

_____

_____

_____

- Are not afraid of causing a RIOT in order to make a difference in this world.

_____

_____

_____

- Would like to receive a REWARD for making a difference in this world.

_____

_____

_____

4. How do the qualifications of the Risky Radicals that the LORD is looking for line up with your present qualifications? What changes do you feel need to be made in your life for there to be a match?

_____

_____

_____

Battalion of Believers

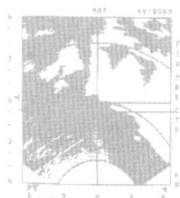

Lesson 5

THROUGHOUT THIS STUDY, WE'VE DISCUSSED THE FACT THAT GOD has a purpose for each and every Christian. Hopefully by now you've been inspired and challenged to step out of a life of mediocre Christianity and into a life of fulfillment and destiny that awaits all those who have the courage to follow God's plan for their lives.

Big God. Big plan. Big picture.

But His plan extends way beyond our individual lives. It's the plan of the ages that existed in the heart and mind of God before time began. It's a BIG plan from a BIG God.

That reminds me of a young guy I once heard preach a message about 'God is Big.' I don't think the kid had ever preached before. His whole message went something like this, "I want to talk to you about how big God is. Man guys, God is BIG. He is SO big. You're not going to believe how BIG God is. He's just BIGGER than anything. He's just BIG..." He went on like that for about twenty minutes, saying the same thing over and over. Then he closed it. The funny thing about it is, twenty-five years later I still remember his message.

I often tell people to step back and look at the BIG picture, because doing so will help put their present circumstances into perspective. It's like the proverbial, "can't see the forest for the trees" syndrome. At times we all need to step back, look up, and let the Lord *open the eyes of our understanding* (Ephesians 1:18).

That's the purpose of this lesson, *Battalion of Believers* – to lift your vision beyond what's going on in *your* world so you can catch hold of God's master plan of the ages and discover how you have a part in that plan.

This is a serious word that's relevant to every single believer. I believe that it will stir something up inside you that's lying dormant. And if you're in the midst of a battle, I believe it will strengthen you so that you can keep fighting and not faint.

America's Slippery Slide

God's Battalion of Believers is a company of warriors who are deeply concerned about and committed to the cause of the Lord. What's important to God is important to us. What thrills His heart, thrills our hearts. What makes Him angry, makes us angry. What causes His heart pain, hurts our hearts, too. What grieves Him, also grieves us.

That's why there's something gnawing at me that should be gnawing at you, too. I'm deeply disturbed about the condition of this nation. With an evangelical church on every corner, why is it that our country is more steeped in sin than ever before? Or how can it be that the Bible belt leads the nation in murders? And with the freedom that we have in this nation to preach salvation through Jesus Christ, why is it that America is unsaved?

> America slips further towards judgment as the Church slips further from God.

While it's true that Christians seem to be a little agitated when homosexuals wed and kiss on the evening news, they quickly brush this away and fall back into their lives of ease. America slips further towards judgment as the church slips further from God.

When I look at how it all began and compare it with how things are going today, my heart is grieved. Something must change!

We must determine in our hearts that it is time to raise the standard. We *must* mount a counterattack against the complacent curse that is coming against the Church in America.

All my life, people have asked me why I work so hard. "Slow down, brother. Just slow down," they tell me. And I say, "What do you mean, 'slow down'? Everybody around here is working at a snail's pace while the devil is working overtime." Here's the Church – work an hour, sleep 23 hours. Work another hour, sleep 23 hours. And while the Church is sleeping, the world around us is dying and going to hell.

Time is *not* on our side. It's as if the sun is setting, and the harvest is still ripe in the fields. We must do everything within our means to show our Lord that we take seriously His Great Commission. And, we must challenge each other to do what must be done according to Hebrews 10:23-4,

> *Let us hold fast the confession of our hope without wavering, for He who promised is faithful. And let us consider one another in order to stir up love and good works...*

How Did It All Begin?

When I look at how Christianity began and compare it to how things are today, my heart is grieved. How did this whole thing called Christianity begin? What was the result of the Lord Jesus and His teaching on earth? What was the response of His no-compromise, in-your-face, religion ruffling, heart-rending, conscious-piercing words of love? We know what the response was. Luke 23:5 tells us that, *"they were the more fierce, saying, He stirreth up the people..."*

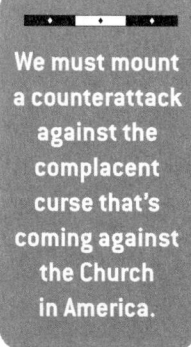

We must mount a counterattack against the complacent curse that's coming against the Church in America.

Jesus stirred up the people. He caused some problems. And then He passed that on to His disciples. The Bible says in Acts 17:6 that they turned the world upside down. In Acts 24:5, they said that Paul was a pest.

> For we have found this man a pestilent fellow, and a mover of sedition among all the Jews throughout the world, and a ringleader of the sect of the Nazarenes...

I love that. Paul was bothersome. Always in everyone else's affairs. Always preaching the Gospel and telling people that they needed to be saved through Jesus.

What a far cry that is from the Church today! What do I mean by that? Here's what I believe about the Church in America. The devil is not concerned about Sunday morning. In fact, I believe he's working overtime every Sunday morning, waking people up to go to church. Why? Because the devil knows that if he can get America into that stained-glass building, and they can get their little sermonette and scratch their little religious itch (you know, the "we've-got-to-feel-good-about-that-little-'spiritual'-part-of-our-lives"); if he can get them in and out of church in a hurry (in some churches, the message is twelve minutes long and the whole service is just 45 minutes), then they'll stay in their little religious bubble, thinking everything is okay.

Whatever happened to *"denying ourselves; picking up our cross, and following Him"*? Whatever happened to solid preaching on sin and repentance? When was the last time you heard a pastor preach a **bold** sermon on a **hot** hell?

> When was the last time you heard a pastor preach a bold sermon on a hot hell?

Jesus gave His diciples the pattern for us to follow. And it is no different for us today. Jesus and His disciples stirred things up wherever they went. Because of their courage and their determination to preach and obey the truth, they changed the world and the course of history itself.

I've made a choice. I don't want to go through life not having affected my community, our nation, and the world in which we live. I want to make a *difference* in this world. How about you?

I have a thick book at home that is full of documented statistics of what life was like in England before and after John Wesley. Think about it. The reason S. Wesley Bready wrote a book entitled *England, Before and After Wesley* was because Wesley's influence literally changed that nation!

If one person could affect a nation so powerfully, can you imagine what God could do with a mighty *Battalion of Believers* who are holy, anointed, and totally committed to His cause? I'm asking God to raise up such a battalion.

A *battalion* is a tactical military unit of any size, with a headquarters, infantry, and artillery.

I'm asking God to raise up a battalion of believers:

1. Who are a THREAT to the kingdom of darkness.

Do you want to know what a threat is? A threat is *an expression of intention of danger.* I want to be a *threat* to the kingdom of darkness!

To be a threat to the devil's kingdom, we must take an active, aggressive stand and declare, "Satan, we give you notice. We are NOT playing games. We've had it with you stealing our children and corrupting our society. We've had it with all the trash that you are pouring out across the television and the Internet… we've had it!"

Are you a threat to the kingdom of darkness? Are you running from the devil or is he running from you? Do you constantly cower to his power, or does the devil cower at the power that's operating in you?

> I've made a choice. I don't want to go through life not having affected my community, our nation, and the world in which we live.

All Jesus had to do was show up on the scene and the demons would tremble. Look at what happened the day Jesus went to the Gergesenes.

> *And when he was come to the other side into the country of the Gergesenes, there met him two possessed with devils, coming out of the tombs, exceeding fierce, so that no man might pass by that way.*
>
> *And, behold, they cried out, saying, "What have we to do with thee, Jesus, thou Son of God?* **art thou come hither to torment us before the time?** *" And there was a good way off from them an herd of many swine feeding. So the devils besought him, saying, "If thou cast us out, suffer us to go away into the herd of swine."*
>
> *And he said unto them, 'Go.' And when they were come out, they went into the herd of swine: and, behold, the whole herd of swine ran violently down a steep place into the sea, and perished in the waters.*
>
> *And they that kept them fled, and went their ways into the city, and told every thing, and what was befallen to the possessed of the devils.*
>
> *And, behold, the whole city came out to meet Jesus: and when they saw him, they besought him that he would depart out of their coasts.*
> *(Matthew 8:28-34)*

When Jesus cast the demons out of the possessed men and into the herd of swine, the whole city freaked out and begged Him to leave!

I want it to be said of me, "What have we to do with you, Steve Hill? Have you come to Dallas/Ft. Worth to torment us before our time?" They should say the same about you, too.

Who Are You?

How about the account of the seven sons of Sceva? These men saw Paul and others casting out demons, so they decided to try it. The only problem was that they were not in a right relationship with Jesus Christ. So this one demon leaped on the seven men and overcame them, causing them to flee out of the house naked and wounded!

> *Then certain of the vagabond Jews, exorcists, took upon them to call over them which had evil spirits the name of the Lord Jesus, saying, "We adjure you by Jesus whom Paul preacheth." And there were seven sons of one Sceva, a Jew, and chief of the priests, which did so. And the evil spirit answered and said, "Jesus I know, and Paul I know; but who are ye?" And the man in whom the evil spirit was leaped on them, and overcame them, and prevailed against them, so that they fled out of that house naked and wounded.*
>
> *And this was known to all the Jews and Greeks also dwelling at Ephesus; and fear fell on them all, and the name of the Lord Jesus was magnified.*
>
> *And many that believed came, and confessed, and shewed their deeds. Many of them also which used curious arts brought their books together, and burned them before all men: and they counted the price of them, and found it fifty thousand pieces of silver. So mightily grew the word of God and prevailed.*
> *(Acts 19:13-20)*

What's especially interesting to me about this account is what the demon said to the sons of Sceva, *"Jesus I know and Paul I know; but who are you?"*

I remember the first time the devil said that to me when I was about to cast a demon out of a demon-possessed person. I had been a Christian for just about a year. And the demon said, "Jesus I know. Paul I know, but who are you?" I rose up and answered, "My name is Steve Hill and I've been washed in the blood of the lamb and in the name of Jesus Christ of Nazareth. Satan, I bind you. Loose her and let her go..." "Oh, that's who you are..." "You'd better believe it! Now go!" And it went!

My friend, does the devil tremble when you step into a room, or does he kick back in his lazy boy and say, "Oh, it's just Bob." Or, "That's just Susie. She's not living for God. She's in and out"?

YOU Can Do Something About The Devil

You can do something about the kingdom of darkness. How? You invade it with light! The light dispels the darkness.

Have you ever been in a pitch-dark room and someone lit a match? The entire focus of everyone in the room is on that light. All you can see is that light. How powerful is the light of just *one Christian* who walks into the world of darkness!

Leonard Ravenhill used to tell me, "Steve, I don't care if your name is in every Christian periodical in the nation. It doesn't matter to me if you are in *Charisma* or *Christianity Today*, or in *Newsweek* and *The New York Times*. I don't care if you are on *CNN* or *Good Morning, America*..." Little did he know that

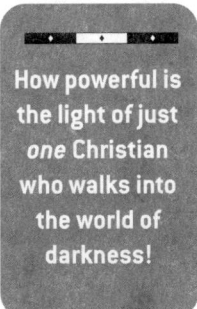

How powerful is the light of just *one* Christian who walks into the world of darkness!

he was prophesying, because every bit of what he said came to pass and more. He said, "It doesn't make any difference who knows your name here on earth. I want to know one thing. Are you known in hell? Are you on the devil's Ten Most Wanted list? Are you one of those that causes demons to tremble?"

He was telling me, "Steve, hell takes note of a holy man of God who is determined to make a difference in this world for God. Such a man is a powerful, mighty weapon in His hands, known of God and known in hell..."

Here's how you become a threat to the kingdom of darkness:

Allow Jesus to <u>SAVE</u> you by His power...

That if thou shalt confess with thy mouth the Lord Jesus, and shalt believe in thine heart that God hath raised him from the dead, thou shalt be saved. For with the heart man believeth unto righteousness; and with the mouth confession is made unto salvation. (Romans 10:9-10)

Allow Jesus to <u>SANCTIFY</u> you with His Word...

Sanctify them through thy truth: thy word is truth. (John 17:17)

Allow Jesus to <u>SATURATE</u> you with His Spirit...

But ye shall receive power, after that the Holy Ghost is come upon you: and ye shall be witnesses unto me both in Jerusalem, and in all Judaea, and in Samaria, and unto the uttermost part of the earth. (Acts 1:8)

Allow Jesus to <u>SEND</u> you with His anointing...

The Spirit of the Lord is upon me, because he hath anointed me to preach the gospel to the poor; he hath sent me to heal the brokenhearted, to preach deliverance to the captives, and recovering of sight to the blind, to set at liberty them that are bruised, to preach the acceptable year of the Lord. (Luke 4:18-19)

My friend, no devil can stand against a person who is saved, sanctified, saturated with the Spirit, and sent with His anointing!

I'm asking God to raise up a battalion of believers:

2. Who will not TOLERATE the sins of the saints.

When I mention the word "sins," most of us automatically think of drinking, cussing, pornography and all of the hideous things which so many of us used to do. But little do we realize that as we're sailing on our way to heaven in this boat called Christianity, there are other sins in our lives that grieve God and cause Him pain.

One of these sins of the saints is:

Lack of Faith

Remember what Jesus said to the men on the road to Emmaus in Luke 24:25? "*O foolish ones, and slow of heart to believe in all that the prophets have spoken.*" Another time, Jesus rebuked His disciples who were in the boat with Him saying, "*Why are you fearful, O you of little faith?*" (Matthew 8:26)

In both of these situations, Jesus was rebuking His disciples for their lack of faith, not unbelievers. The Word also tells us that *whatever is not from faith is sin* (Romans 14:23).

I want to be one of those childlike faith people that Jesus commends. When He has a special assignment, I want Him to be able to say, "Steve will do it. He believes Me for all things ..." How about you?

Let me address this issue of faith at bit further, right where we live. What kind of faith do you have for your church? When the pastor announces that there are miracles in the making concerning the church, do you get on board and join your faith with him to see it come to pass? Or do you sit back, add your two cents worth of doubt and unbelief, and say, "Man, there's no way that's going to happen."

What kind of faith do you have when I announce that we're going to open up a Bible school to train up thousands of men and women, and send them all over the world to preach the Gospel? Do you have a hard time fathoming it? Or, do you grab hold of the vision by faith and embrace it with your heart saying, "How can I be a part of this?"

Who knows, perhaps that Bible School is an answer to your prayers, but you don't even know it yet. Maybe your backslidden son will have a powerful encounter with God during one of our summer revival services and get so on fire that he decides to answer the call of God upon his life. The next thing you know, he's enrolled in that new Bible school, and your whole family has been dramatically affected because we stepped out to believe God for great things.

Remember my friend, Ulf Eckman, who stepped out in faith to plant a thousand churches in Russia at the same time he was building a 5,000-seat sanctuary back in Sweden? He started building that sanctuary when he had only 200 people in his church. The news media blasted him, people came to his house, threw stuff at his car, broke windows and threaten him. Did that deter him? No, because Ulf has mountain-moving faith! He knows that his God is not up in heaven counting pennies. That He owns all the gold and the silver. That He's just looking for someone who will step out in faith and believe Him...

All the while God was looking down at Ulf saying, "My, my, my. What do I have here? Could it be that I've found another Elijah? Could it be that I've found a Moses, or a Noah?"

The story doesn't end there. Today, Ulf is making plans to get into India. Not Southern India where most missionaries go because there's not as much persecution. Ulf wants to go to Northern India where it's tough, and plant a large evangelistic church in every single major city. And by the grace of God, he's going to do it!

By the way, that church in Sweden that Ulf raised up that used to get heckled and harassed, they sowed a missions offering

> There's a great move of God in front of us. It will come through those who are humble.

of $100,000 dollars to help us plant Heartland Fellowship Church!

One more important thing about faith. The Bible says that you demonstrate your faith by your works. James says it this way,

Shew me thy faith without thy works, and
I will shew thee my faith by my works.
(James 2:18b)

Your faith, according to James, is revealed by your works! God's mighty Battalion of Believers is going to be known for their tremendous works produced by mountain-moving faith!

Lack of Humility

One day the disciples came to the Lord and asked Him who was the greatest in the kingdom of heaven. I love how Jesus answered them:

At that time the disciples came to Jesus and asked, "Who is the greatest in the kingdom of heaven?" He called a little child and had him stand among them. And he said: "I tell you the truth, unless you change and become like little children, you will never enter the kingdom of heaven. Therefore, whoever humbles himself like this child is the greatest in the kingdom of heaven."   *(Matthew 18:1-4)*

Jesus' answer, *"Whoever humbles himself like this child is the greatest in the kingdom of heaven,"* must have totally caught the disciples off guard. Like a mirror, His answer exposed their hearts and revealed how contrary their thinking was to God's thinking. We're no different today.

To become greatest, we must humble ourselves and become the least. How opposite that is to the way of the world and to our own natural thinking.

I've had every accolade put on me that a man could stand. It's an eerie, freaky, sickening feeling. Why? Because I know where I came from. I know that it is by the grace of God that I'm breathing. So I don't care who gets the credit.

I believe there is a great move of God in front of us. In the next move of God, the Lord will not only use the clergy, but will mightily use lay people. Regardless of who He chooses to use, it will come through those who are humble.

Humility says, "Pastor, is there any way I can serve? I'm here to help..." Or, "Pastor, I have this gift, this ability...if there's any way you can use this gift, here it is..." Humility rejoices when other people are honored and promoted. Humility is happy to serve in secret where no one sees, and where there is no public honor or recognition...

Some people just set themselves up to get hurt. They get bent out of shape because the pastor didn't take their idea and run with it, or because they weren't selected to serve on a particular committee, or because they weren't selected to sing the solo for Easter.

My friend, here's a piece of advice that if heeded, can save you years of problems. If and when things don't go the way you had hoped, if you'd just take the low seat, keep a right heart, and refuse to get offended, God will cause everything to work out for your good! (Romans 8:28)

Tears and Brokenness

The world is turned off by the prideful, arrogant attitude displayed by so many Christians. Do you know what they are waiting to see? Tears and brokenness.

I'm reminded of the woman with the alabaster box. There was only one way she could get the precious and costly ointment out of the alabaster box so that she could use it to minister to Jesus. She had to break the box. Look at what happened when she did.

And being in Bethany in the house of Simon the leper, as he sat at meat, there came a woman having an alabaster box of ointment of spikenard very precious; and she brake the box, and poured it on his head. (Mark 14:3)

Then took Mary a pound of ointment of spikenard, very costly, and anointed the feet of Jesus, and wiped his feet with her hair: and the house was filled with the odour of the ointment. (John 12:3)

Mary broke open the alabaster box and poured the costly ointment upon the Lord as an act of worship. As she loved on Him and ministered to Him, something else happened – *the whole house* was filled with the aroma of that sweet, costly perfume. Her act of worship touched and affected everyone around her, and changed the atmosphere of the entire house.

My friend, the alabaster box represents our hearts and lives. Within each and every believer resides the most valuable and costly of all treasure, Christ. "*We have this treasure in earthen vessels*" (2 Corinthians 4:7). As we, in brokenness and humility lay down our lives as an act of worship to the Lord, the sweet fragrance of Jesus touches everyone around us and changes lives.

This, my friend, is what the world is waiting for...

Lack of Love

God's *Battalion of Believers* will not tolerate a lack of love. Jesus commanded us to *love one another as He loved us.* It's not just an option or a good idea. It's a command. Therefore, to not love one another is not just an act of disobedience; it's a sin.

My command is this: Love each other as I have loved you. (John 15:12, NIV)

It's one thing to *know* His command to love. It's quite another thing to *live* it. It's one thing to love those who love you. But it's not so easy to love those who don't even like you or who rub you the wrong way.

We would do well to extend to *others* the same kindness, tolerance and patience that the Lord has shown to *us*. Otherwise, we may be in danger of showing contempt for the riches of His kindness as warned in Romans 2:1-4,

> *You, therefore, have no excuse, you who pass judgment on someone else, for at whatever point you judge the other, you are condemning yourself, because you who pass judgment do the same things. Now we know that God's judgment against those who do such things is based on truth. So when you, a mere man, pass judgment on them and yet do the same things, do you think you will escape God's judgment? Or do you show contempt for the riches of his kindness, tolerance and patience, not realizing that God's kindness leads you toward repentance?*

Love's Litmus Test

Why is walking in love so important? First and foremost, because it's a command. But there are other reasons, too. Jesus told us that *the world will know we are His disciples by our love for one another* (John 13:35), so love is important in reaching the lost. And love is essential to our spiritual health and well-being.

Using I Corinthians 13, we can readily see the fruit of *not* walking in love: being impatient. Unkind. Envious. Boastful. Proud. Rude. Self-seeking. Angry. Hold grudges. Delight in evil. Dishonest. Disloyal. Mistrust. Unbelief. Easily gives up. Failure.

Sounds like the world, doesn't it? Sad to say, it sounds like a lot of believers, too.

The Holy Spirit through James takes it a step further by admonishing us about the unruly nature of the tongue. *How can believers use their tongues to bless God, and then turn around and curse men who are made in God's image?* He sums it up by saying, *my brethren, these things ought not to be so.* (James 3:9-10)

Proverbs 18:21 tells us that *death and life are in the power of the tongue.* Did you know that hardly a day goes by that there's not some type of curse spoken over you? It's simply the spirit of the world and age we live in. That's why as Senior Pastor of Heartland Fellowship Church, I conclude every service by speaking a blessing from the Word of God over our people. The results of this blessing have been remarkable.

I Corinthians 13 gives us a great litmus test for measuring our love walk. I love how it reads in the Amplified version.

Love endures long and is patient and kind;
Love never is envious nor boils over with jealousy,
Love is not boastful or vainglorious,
Love does not display itself haughtily.
It is not conceited (arrogant and inflated with pride);
It is not rude (unmannerly) and does not act unbecomingly.
Love (God's love in us) does not insist on its own rights
or its own way, for it is not self-seeking;
It is not touchy or fretful or resentful;
It takes no account of the evil done to it
[it pays no attention to a suffered wrong].
It does not rejoice at injustice and unrighteousness,
but rejoices when right and truth prevail.
Love bears up under anything and everything that comes,
Love is ever ready to believe the best of every person,
Its hopes are fadeless under all circumstances,
and it endures everything [without weakening].
Love never fails [never fades out or becomes obsolete or
comes to an end].
(I Corinthians 13:4-8, Amplified)

In Jude 21, we are instructed to *keep ourselves in the love of God.* One minister used to say it this way, "Every step out of love is sin." Thank God, when we miss the mark by stepping *out* of love, we can immediately repent, receive forgiveness and cleansing through the blood of Jesus, and step right back *into* love.

Every step out of love is sin

The mighty Battalion of Believers that God is raising up today will be known for *following the way of love* (I Corinthians 14:1, NIV). I encourage you to continually apply the measuring rod of I Corinthians 13 to your life and ask yourself each day, "How's my love walk?"

Lack of Unity

Just mention the word "unity" and some people get uncomfortable. All of us have been hurt by others at one time or another. You might as well just accept and get over the fact that for everyone who praises you, there is going to be someone who talks behind your back.

"*How good and pleasant it is for brethren to dwell together in unity…*" According to Psalm 133:1, unity is *good* and *pleasant*. And, if you're going to be a part of God's mighty battalion of believers, it's a necessity.

What do you think a morning is like for our troops fighting terrorism? It would not be uncommon for a scenario like this to happen. An officer stands before his troops who are all standing at attention and says, "Men, yesterday was a tough day. We lost five. Some of you lost your friends…" And these soldiers, many of whom are just eighteen or nineteen years old, start to choke up on the inside. They just saw their best buddy get his head blown off by enemy fire the day before. They're hurting inside. But their standing straight and tall like a soldier.

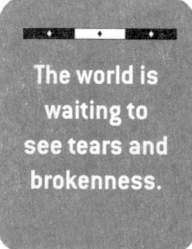

The world is waiting to see tears and brokenness.

Their commanding officer continues, "Today could be worse. The enemy is hiding behind every wall, behind every window. Everywhere you step, there could be a land mine. This could be your last day..."

What do you think it's like for those dedicated men and women? Do you think the commanding officer can stand before his troops and say, "How do you feel? Do you all feel good? We're going to have a great day. Look, the sun is shining. Turn to your neighbor and say, 'I feel good...'" Most assuredly not!

Forgive me my friend, but we need a bit more of this gutsy, "Straighten-up, people-are-dying, the-devil-is-stealing-our-kids, this-is-war," mentality, instead of this "I-want-you-to-make-me-feel-good" type thinking that's so prevalent among Christians today.

Out there on the real battlefield, soldiers set their differences aside. They get in the trenches together, and turn their energy on fighting the *real* enemy instead of each other. This is what God is looking for in those who will be part of His mighty battalion.

I'm reminded of the story of the Tower of Babel found in Genesis chapter 11.

> *And the whole earth was of one language, and of one speech... And they said, "Go to, let us build us a city and a tower, whose top may reach unto heaven; and let us make us a name, lest we be scattered abroad upon the face of the whole earth." And the LORD came down to see the city and the tower, which the children of men builded. And the LORD said, "Behold, the people is one, and they have all one language; and this they begin to do: and now nothing will be restrained from them, which they have imagined to do. Go to, let us go down, and there confound their language, that they may not understand one another's speech."*
>
> *So the LORD scattered them abroad from thence upon the face of all the earth: and they left off to build the city.*

The people were unified together for an ungodly purpose. The Lord knew that if they remained one in purpose and language, that nothing would be restrained from them that they had intended to do. So He broke up their "unholy unity" by confounding their language.

My friend, this story speaks volumes to us about the power and the importance of unity. Oh what God could do with a mighty battalion of believers who are determined to walk in unity! I'm asking God to raise up such a battalion!

The Little Foxes

Lack of faith, lack of humility, lack of love, and lack of unity. Some people may ask, "But Pastor Steve, why are you calling these things sin?" What do you want to call them? A fluffy mistake? Shortcomings? Weaknesses? Down-fallings or areas that we just need to work on? No, my friend, we need to call them what they are: S-I-N. SIN.

"But Pastor Steve, they're just 'little sins.' Everybody has them. What's the big deal?"

Let me show you what the Bible has to say about these so-called "little sins." In the Song of Solomon these "little sins" are referred to as "little foxes":

> *Catch the foxes for us, The little foxes that are ruining the vineyards, While our vineyards are in blossom.* (Song of Solomon 2:15, NASB)

I've studied foxes. They're very smart. They'll sit still and wait all day for the keeper of the vineyard to leave his post. Maybe the vineyard keeper decides to take a short lunch break, or a quick little nap. Whatever the case, the fox will lay and wait all day for just that moment. As soon as the keeper is gone, the fox not only helps itself to the grapes, but he gnaws at the vine itself, ultimately destroying it.

What does that mean to us? My friend, the things that we might think of as 'little sins' are the very thing that destroy not only our fruitfulness but even our lives. This is why we're told to *"catch the little foxes."*

God is searching for a company of believers who will rise up and not permit the *"little foxes"* to spoil His precious vineyards.

I'm asking God to raise up a battalion of believers:

3. Who will not become distracted from the TASK that is set before them.

Brethren, we have a job to do. It's not hazy. It's not difficult to understand. It's very clear.

Jesus told us to *"Go ye therefore, and teach all nations, baptizing them in the name of the Father, and of the Son, and of the Holy Ghost: Teaching them to observe all things whatsoever I have commanded you: and, lo, I am with you alway, even unto the end of the world. Amen"* (Matthew 28:19-20).

He said, "Go and teach all nations." Not, "Get on your knees and pray about it."

Do you know why I think Jesus didn't say to pray about going? Because He knew that most would say, "Jesus, give me three dreams and a vision, then I'll know it's You. Then I'll go..." Consequently, they stay.

The Bible does say to pray without ceasing, and I'm a prayer warrior who loves to pray. But sometimes people use prayer as an excuse to not obey what's plainly written in the Word. Jesus said, "Go." Period.

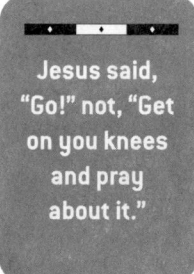

Jesus said, "Go!" not, "Get on you knees and pray about it."

Here's a powerful portion of scripture concerning the work of the Lord, where Jesus calls people to follow Him. Look at the many excuses they gave to justify not following Him:

Now it happened as they journeyed on the road, that someone said to Him,

"Lord, I will follow You wherever You go." And Jesus said to him, "Foxes have holes and birds of the air have nests, but the Son of Man has nowhere to lay His head." Then He said to another, "Follow Me." But he said, "Lord, let me first go and bury my father." Jesus said to him, "let the dead bury their own dead, but you go and preach the kingdom of God."
(Luke 9:57-60)

Jesus wasn't diminishing the importance of family. No, He was emphasizing the fact that once you get involved in the work of the Lord, you must set your eye on the cross, put that plow in the furrow, and keep moving forward. If you turn to the right or left, you are going to get off track and miss what God has for you.

This is why Jeri and I have been able to do so much for God over the years. When God gives us a mandate, we do what He tells us to do. When He tells us, "Step right *there*," we do what He tells us to do. We don't get distracted from the assignment, even when well-meaning people try to persuade us to do something else. We finish the job and then move to the next assignment. We've done that all over the world, and that's one of the reasons the Lord has blessed the work of our hands the way that He has. He can count on us to stay the course and finish the tasks that He gives us to do.

I'm asking God to raise up a battalion of believers:

4. That is willing to be TRAINED to do the work of the ministry.

No matter what we've done for the Lord or how much good we've accomplished over the years, *none* of us have graduated from the School of God. There's *always* more to learn.

None of us have graduated from the School of God. We should never stop learning.

I promise you, in these last days the devil is going to pull out every weapon he has to try to thwart the purpose and plan of God. So the question for us is, are we willing to be trained in the things of God to take victory in this war?

God has a strategy for every battle we face, just like He did for the children of Israel. Have you ever noticed that the children of Israel could never count on yesterday's strategy to fight today's battle. Consider this:

Only one time did the Lord part the Red Sea, and then close it up on their enemies.

Only one time did the Lord select 300 soldiers to defeat an entire army via lapping water.

Only one time did they win a war as Aaron and Hur held up Moses' arms.

Only one time did the Lord have them march around the walls of a city for seven days to see the city walls come tumbling down.

Only one time did Israel defeat the Philistines with a slingshot and a smooth stone.

One time the Lord told David to face the enemy head on, but the next time He told David to circle behind the enemy and attack them in front of the mulberry trees when they heard the sound of marching in the tree tops (2 Samuel 5:17-25).

One of the reasons the Lord put these stories in the Bible is so that we'd learn the important of obtaining today's strategy for today's battle. We must continually depend upon Him.

The Big Picture

I happened to fly over the Mississippi River when it flooded awhile back. Do you know what I found? It was one thing to view the flood from the ground or even from television. But it was another thing entirely to view the flood from an airplane. From up above, I could see where the waters had overrun the bank, and I could see clearly the places that had been affected by the flood. It was amazing how I saw things differently from up above. I could clearly see the big picture.

My friend, God has this perspective. He is up above looking down at your life. He sees everything about your life – past, present, and future – down to the minutest detail. He sees the big picture.

Sometimes you may be heading a certain direction and God puts something right in your path to turn you a different direction. Why? Because He doesn't want you to go over that mountain. He's got another path for you. He sees what's up ahead. He sees the enemy's camp across the mountain. He knows what the devil is planning.

This is why I get before Him every day and ask Him to teach me and guide me. I know that He sees the big picture and He knows everything. This is also why I'm so easily trained by God. Because I endeavor to be teachable, and I depend upon Him to guide me. I'm not speaking as someone who has arrived, but rather as a fellow pilgrim who has learned some valuable lessons.

Look at His incredible promise to us found in Psalm 32:8,

> *I will instruct you and teach you in the way you should go; I will guide you with My eye...*

How I love that! As we let the Lord instruct us and teach us in the way that we should go, He will most assuredly guide us with His all-seeing, all-knowing eye!

I'm asking God to raise up a battalion of believers:

5. Who can be TRUSTED in the heat of battle.

There was a time when Jeremiah complained to the Lord about the prosperity of the wicked. Look at the Lord's response to his complaint.

If thou hast run with the footmen, and they have wearied thee, then how canst thou contend with horses? And if in the land of peace, wherein thou trustedst, they wearied thee, then how wilt thou do in the swelling of Jordan? (Jeremiah 12:5)

The Lord was telling him, "Jeremiah, the prosperity of the wicked is a small thing in My eyes – I'm a big God. But if the smallest thing that you're exposed to wears you out, what's going to happen when you're exposed to something major?"

"If you can't handle things when times are good and the sun is shining, what are you going to do when the Jordan River swells during the rainy season?"

Back then, when the Jordan River would flood, the wild beasts were driven from where they lived alongside the river to the farmlands, creating incredible havoc, killing men, and devouring cattle and sheep.

I don't know what's going to happen in America, but I know that God is not going to let this country just keep on openly committing abominations. What if our nation goes through a shaking like it has never experienced before? If you can't handle life when times are good, what are you going to do when the hard times come and the floodwaters rise?

My friend, it's easy to serve the Lord during the good times when the sun is shining. But it's a whole different ballgame when you are out there being shot at and you've got a few bullet holes in you. Are you going to serve the Lord then?

During the height of the Pensacola Revival, an assistant principle from one of the public schools began to bring hundreds of spiritually hungry students to the revival. As a result, many of them were being powerfully saved. The fire of God was spreading throughout that public school!

> A soldier's true value is found on the battlefield during the heat of battle.

Some parents began to complain because their kids were getting radical for Jesus, so the assistant principle was brought before the school board and given an ultimatum. Either he stopped bringing those kids to the revival, or he would be fired.

So the assistant principle had to make a decision. Would he risk his job and continue to take the kids to the revival to get them saved? Or would he opt for security, and comply with the demands of the school board, and be held accountable to God for the souls of those kids? He decided to continue taking the kids to the revival, and he lost his job. He lost everything.

The impact of his decision was so powerful that a team of reporters from 20/20 flew in and did a story on him. During the interview 20/20 asked him, "If you have to do it all over again, what changes would you make?" He said, "Absolutely none. I would do the exact same thing."

I got a letter from him recently. He cited an incident that made national headlines. A student from his former school poured gasoline all over himself and lit his body. "Who knows," he wrote, "If I'd been able to continue to bring students to the revival, perhaps that kid would have found the Lord and never doused himself in gasoline…"

Heaven only knows, but one thing is for sure. This man could be trusted in the heat of battle. The Lord counted him faithful in the face of fiery persecution.

It's easy to say that you can be trusted to stand when everything's going good. But what about in the heat of battle? The disciples thought they could handle it, too. But in the Garden of Gethsemane, during Jesus' darkest hour when He needed them the most, they slept. "Could you not watch with Me one hour? Could you not just help Me out for one hour, boys?" (Matthew 26:36-46) Just one hour…

Remember, soldiers are not tested in the barracks. A soldier's true value is found on the battlefield during the heat of battle. Can God count on you in the heat of the

> Unless you go through some trials and tribulations, you're never going to become a soldier. It's called the making of a man or woman of God.

battle? Unless you go through some trials and tribulations, you're never going to become a soldier. It's called the making of a man or woman of God, and it's part of the training process for His battalion of believers.

I'm asking God to raise up a battalion of believers:

6. Who will not waiver from the TRUTH, regardless of the circumstances.

I've watched churches back off from the truth. You don't back off from the truth by not believing it. You back off by not preaching it anymore. In most pulpits today, you will be hard-pressed to hear any preaching that has to do with the sin that separates man from God.

Jesus prayed to the Father, "*Sanctify them through thy truth: thy word is truth.*" (John 17:17)

What is truth?

That man is a sinner (Romans 3:23)
That man is separated from God because of sin (Isaiah 59:2)
That sin will destroy you (Romans 6:23)
That sin will enslave you (John 8:34)
That sin will keep you from heaven (I Corinthians 6:9-10)
That the gift of God is eternal life through Jesus Christ our Lord (Romans 6:23)
That the only way you can be saved is by faith in Jesus Christ (Romans 10:9-10
There is only one way to heaven (John 14:6)
That the gift of God is eternal life through Jesus Christ our Lord (Romans 6:23)
That once you become a Christian, your life changes (2 Corinthians 5:17)

My friend, these truths are non-negotiable. There's no gray area. What do you believe? Are you willing to stand for the truth no matter what? If so, then you will not flinch if and when a reporter ever sticks a microphone in your face and says, "We hear that your church preaches against sin. Would you name some of those sins?"

Then you'll boldly open your mouth and declare what the Bible says, knowing full well that the reporter will turn on you and mischaracterize you as a hatemonger who divides and hates people, simply because you stood for the Truth.

We should learn from Billy Graham's example. For years, he's always answered those type of questions with, "The Bible says..." and it has served him well. To do that, however, you must know what you believe. You must know the Truth.

I'm asking God to raise up a battalion of believers:

7. That is determined to TRIUMPH victoriously over the enemy.

When Goliath uttered his proud, arrogant, death threats against David, notice what David did *not* do. He did *not* heed Goliath's threats. He did *not* get someone else to fight his battle. He *didn't* use Saul's armor. He *didn't* listen to the criticism of his brothers. He *didn't* judge the outcome of the battle by how things looked. He *didn't* trust in his own strength and ability. He did *not* yield to the fear and intimidation of the enemy. Nor did he retreat.

Instead, David went into the battle *fully determined* to triumph victoriously over the enemy! And he did!

> And when the Philistine looked about, and saw David, he disdained him: for he was but a youth, and ruddy, and of a fair countenance. And the Philistine said unto David, "Am I a dog, that thou comest to me with staves? And the Philistine cursed David by his gods." And the Philistine said to David, "Come

to me, and I will give thy flesh unto the fowls of the air, and to the beasts of the field."

Then said David to the Philistine, "Thou comest to me with a sword, and with a spear, and with a shield: but I come to thee in the name of the LORD of hosts, the God of the armies of Israel, whom thou hast defied. This day will the LORD deliver thee into mine hand; and I will smite thee, and take thine head from thee; and I will give the carcases of the host of the Philistines this day unto the fowls of the air, and to the wild beasts of the earth; that all the earth may know that there is a God in Israel. And all this assembly shall know that the LORD saveth not with sword and spear: for the battle is the LORD'S, and he will give you into our hands."

And it came to pass, when the Philistine arose, and came and drew nigh to meet David, that David hasted, and ran toward the army to meet the Philistine. And David put his hand in his bag, and took thence a stone, and slang it, and smote the Philistine in his forehead, that the stone sunk into his forehead; and he fell upon his face to the earth. So David prevailed over the Philistine with a sling and with a stone, and smote the Philistine, and slew him; but there was no sword in the hand of David. Therefore David ran, and stood upon the Philistine, and took his sword, and drew it out of the sheath thereof, and slew him, and cut off his head therewith. And when the Philistines saw their champion was dead, they fled.
(1 Samuel 17:42-51)

When David told Goliath, "...This day will the LORD deliver thee into mine hand; and I will smite thee, and take thine head from thee," he was saying, "I'm not *trying* to be successful, Goliath. I *am* successful! I'm not *trying* to conquer. I am *more* than a conqueror!" David knew his God. He walked with Him. He had a relationship with Him. He'd experienced God's delivering hand before, and he was confident that God would deliver him again. *This* is why he could face the enemy head-on and triumph over him.

David didn't just sit down and relax after his great victory over Goliath. He went on to fight many more battles, and to win many great victories.

How did David triumph over his enemies, battle after battle? Was it because he was anointed to be king? Because he was skillful with a slingshot? Or because he had an army of fierce warriors? Or because of his years of experience on the battlefield? While these things may be true, the key to David's continual success in triumphing over his enemy was found in his relationship with the Lord.

David tells us this much in his song of victory and praise found in 2 Samuel 22 where he *"spoke unto the LORD the words of this song in the day that the LORD had delivered him out of the hand of all his enemies, and out of the hand of Saul"* (2 Samuel 22:1).

In this passage you'll find three constants in David's life that led him to victory over and over again. I encourage you to read this passage out loud. As you do, you will hear powerful Words of instruction that will help *you* triumph over all *your* enemies, time and time again.

Here's how David triumphed over all his enemies:

• He *called* upon the Lord

> *"The LORD is my rock, and my fortress, and my deliverer; The God of my rock; in him will I trust: he is my shield, and the horn of my salvation, my high tower, and my refuge, my saviour; thou savest me from violence...I will <u>call</u> on the LORD, who is worthy to be praised: so shall I be saved from mine enemies."* (2 Samuel 22:1-4)

- He kept his hands *clean*

  "...he delivered me, because he delighted in me. The LORD rewarded me according to my righteousness: according to the <u>cleanness</u> of my hands hath he recompensed me. For I have kept the ways of the LORD, and have not wickedly departed from my God. For all his judgments were before me: and as for his statutes, I did not depart from them. I was also upright before him, and have kept myself from mine iniquity. Therefore the LORD hath recompensed me according to my righteousness; according to my cleanness in his eye sight..."   *(2 Samuel 22:20-25)*

- He *consumed* his enemies

  *"...he teacheth my hands to war; so that a bow of steel is broken by mine arms...**I have pursued mine enemies, and destroyed them; and turned not again until I had <u>consumed</u> them.** And I have consumed them, and wounded them, that they could not arise: yea, they are fallen under my feet. For thou hast girded me with strength to battle: them that rose up against me hast thou subdued under me..."*   *(2 Samuel 22:35, 38-40)*

David had learned the secret of how to triumph over his enemies – he *called* upon the Lord, he kept his hands *clean*, then he went forth in faith to *consume* his enemies. Note too, that his victories were not merely personal victories. No, David's victories were also for the nation of Israel and the kingdom of God.

My friend, David's example is in the Bible for *our* sake! He even triumphed over his horrible fall into sin. Personal repentance was a strong part of David's life, and a primary reason why he triumphed over his enemies.

You'll Be Glad You Did

Determine that you are going to be among God's mighty *Battalion of Believers*. Then, on that day when you sit down at the Marriage Supper of the Lamb and you look around that huge table, you're going to be glad where you're sitting. There are going to be stalwart men and women of God at that table like David, the Apostle Paul, Esther, Peter, Elijah, John and Charles Wesley, George Whitfield, Smith Wigglesworth, Leonard Ravenhill, and countless others.

On that day, you'll have something to say to these giants of the faith because you weren't a wimp in Christendom. And best of all, when you stand before Jesus you will hear those words, "Well done, My good and faithful servant!"

Welcome, my friend, to God's mighty *Battalion of Believers*.

Questions for Group Discussion

Discuss the following characteristics of God's *Battalion of Believers* and how they relate to you personally. They:

1. Are a THREAT to the kingdom of darkness.

    (1) SAVED by His power—Romans 10:9-10
    (2) SANCTIFIED with His Word—John 17:17
    (3) SATURATED with His Spirit—Acts1:8
    (4) SENT with His anointing—Luke 4:18-19

    _____

    _____

    _____

    _____

2. Will not TOLERATE the sins of the saints.

    (1) Lack of faith.
    (2) Lack of humility.
    (3) Lack of love.
    (4) Lack of unity.

    _____

    _____

    _____

    _____

3. Will not be distracted from the TASK that is set before them.

    _____

    _____

    _____

    _____

4. Are willing to be TRAINED to do the work of the ministry.

_____

_____

_____

_____

5. Can be TRUSTED in the heat of battle.

_____

_____

_____

_____

6. Will not waiver from the TRUTH, regardless of circumstances.

_____

_____

_____

_____

7. Are determined to TRIUMPH victoriously over the enemy.

   (1) Calling upon the LORD.
   (2) Keeping their hands clean.
   (3) Consuming their enemies.

_____

_____

_____

_____

Take It To The Extreme

Lesson 6

WE LIVE IN A WORLD OF EXTREMISM. *EXTREME* MEANS *VERY INTENSE,* *far beyond the norm. Radical.* It's a word that has become an integral part of today's thrill-seeking society. We often hear of things like extreme adventures, extreme sports, extreme vacations, or extreme roller coasters.

I am one of those who believes in extreme Christianity.

As a Christian, you're not just human. You are superhuman. The Spirit of Christ lives in you and He will enable you to do things that no one has ever dreamed of before.

Awhile back I wrote a book entitled, "Wanted: Extreme Christians." It's all about extreme Christian living. What's sad is that if the Apostle Paul got my book and read it, he'd say, "That's *normal* Christianity, Steve! Why is this called *extreme?*" Yet what should be considered *normal* is often labeled *extreme* by many believers today.

The purpose of this lesson is to inspire and challenge you to go beyond mediocre, status quo Christianity to become everything you can be for Christ.

> What should be considered *normal* is often labeled *extreme* by many believers today.

Extreme Christianity

As believers, God expects every one of us to live our lives to the extreme. Of course, nobody has ever lived a more extreme life than Jesus Christ. From His birth to His baptism, from His message to His miracles, from His life to His love, from His purity to His power, from His cross to His crown – everything Jesus did was extreme.

Just before He left the earth, He turned to His disciples and said, "Boys, go into all the world and preach the Gospel." The mandate that He laid before them was the most powerful, edgy thing they'd ever heard. He told them, "Touch the whole world with what I've taught you these past three years. Take My Word to everybody. Goodbye." And then He took off into heaven. How incredible! How extreme!

Clearly, Jesus didn't shed His blood for the sins of the world so that we could sit back and enjoy a life of comfort and ease. No, He commanded His disciples to reach the whole world with the Gospel, and this same mandate applies to us today.

Jeri and I have been known to do some extreme things for God over the years. When we were in Costa Rica preparing to be missionaries to South America, a man who taught language arts at Fuller Seminary asked our Spanish class one day, "How many want to get radical about your language learning?" Jeri and I both raised our hands. The majority of the two hundred students in the room did not raise their hands because they wanted to learn Spanish in a very controlled classroom setting.

Our instructor then taught us how to say the following phrase in Spanish: "My name is (Steve Hill). I'm in Costa Rica to learn Spanish. I must practice what I learn. Can I come live with you?" After Jeri and I memorized these sentences, we were instructed to get on a city bus and walk from person to person, asking passengers if we could come live with them. Three or four people on the bus said, "Sure, why not!" So we moved in with a family for our remaining time in Costa Rica.

> God expects every one of us to live our lives to the extreme.

136

Initially, they didn't speak English and we didn't speak Spanish, which forced us to learn Spanish quickly. Now that's extreme!

Extremists In The Bible

The Bible is full of men and women who lived extreme lives for God. As I study their lives, I am blown away by the faith they exhibited, and challenged to go beyond the norm in my own life.

Extreme Behavior of a Friend of God

Someone in the Bible whose extreme life has always encouraged me is Abraham. We all remember when he was told by God to go sacrifice his only son, Isaac. Abraham obeyed the Lord, no questions asked. He got his son, loaded up the mule, put wood on it, went three days to the place of sacrifice, laid Isaac on top of the wood, and then lifted up the knife to sacrifice Isaac. At that moment, the angel of the Lord called out and said, "Abraham! Stop! Don't harm the boy. You did good. You obeyed the Lord. There's a ram in the thicket for your sacrifice. Because of your obedience, you've found favor with God."

> *By faith Abraham, when he was tried, offered up Isaac: and he that had received the promises offered up his only begotten son, Of whom it was said, That in Isaac shall thy seed be called: Accounting that God was able to raise him up, even from the dead; from whence also he received him in a figure.* (Hebrews 11:17-19)

> *Was not Abraham our father justified by works, when he had offered Isaac his son upon the altar? Seest thou how faith wrought with his*

works, and by works was faith made perfect? And the scripture was fulfilled which saith, Abraham believed God, and it was imputed unto him for righteousness: and he was called the Friend of God.
(James 2:21-23)

What was God doing? He was testing Abraham. Hebrews 11:17 says that Abraham, when he was tested, offered up Isaac by faith. Because of his extreme act of faith and obedience, Abraham was declared righteous and called the friend of God. Centuries later, he is noted in the "Hall of Faith" and held in a place of honor for his extreme walk with God.

Just like God tested Abraham, at times He will set you up for a similar experience to see what you're made of.

Extreme Behavior That Caused Walls To Tumble

How about Joshua when God told him to march around the walls of Jericho? The Lord said, "Joshua, don't worry about the walls. Just do what I tell you to do and march, march, march around the city for a week. On the last day, march and blow the horn and the walls will come tumbling down." Joshua obeyed, and the walls came tumbling down. Hebrews 11:30 tells us that *"by faith the walls of Jericho fell down, after they were compassed about seven days."*

Do you have any "Jerichos" in your life? I've had plenty. I love "Jerichos," because when the walls come tumbling down, you know that you didn't do it, and so does everyone else.

Extreme Behavior That Receives Miracles

How about the woman with the issue of blood who used her last drop of energy to press through the crowd to touch the hem of His garment? Or the men who lowered their paralytic friend through the roof to get to Jesus? I can just imagine Jesus on a cot somewhere later that night. While the disciples are all snoring, He's lying awake thinking, "Man, that's My kind of extreme behavior. If more people would just believe Me like that..."

Extreme Behavior That Caused Jesus To Marvel

One of my favorite examples of extreme behavior was the centurion who came to Jesus and said, "I need help. My servant is at home sick..." Jesus said unto him, "I will come." Let's stop here and think about this. If I had a need back home and Jesus Christ was to stand in front of me and say , "I'll come over to your house right now to take care of it..." I'd say, "Great, Jesus. Let's go to my house!" Who wouldn't?! But not the centurion. Instead, he said, "No, it's not necessary, Lord. I am a man under authority. You are one of authority. I'm not worthy that You should come under my roof. Just speak the Word and my servant will be healed..."

> And when Jesus was entered into Capernaum, there came unto him a centurion, beseeching him, And saying, "Lord, my servant lieth at home sick of the palsy, grievously tormented." And Jesus saith unto him, "I will come and heal him."
>
> The centurion answered and said, "Lord, I am not worthy that thou shouldest come under my roof: but speak the word only, and my servant shall be healed. For I am a man under authority, having soldiers under me: and I say to this man, Go, and he goeth; and to another, Come, and he cometh; and to my servant, Do this, and he doeth it."
>
> When Jesus heard it, he marvelled, and said to them that followed, "Verily I say unto you, I have not found so great faith, no, not in Israel..." And Jesus said unto the centurion, "Go thy way; and as thou hast believed, so be it

*done unto thee." And his servant was healed in
the selfsame hour.* (Matthew 8:5-10,13)

Did you notice what Jesus said about this man who wasn't
even an Israelite? Jesus marveled and declared that He had not
found so great faith in all of Israel! What a testimony! I want
Jesus to be able to say that about me – that when He has a special
assignment that needs to get done, He can say, "I'm going to
entrust this to Steve because he believes Me and I know I can
count on him…"

The Lord is searching the earth today for those who will
answer the call to live an extreme – radical, beyond the norm
– Christian life. He's looking for those who will choose to go
beyond the baby diaper stage of Christianity to become men and
women of God who know how to fight. Are you one of those who
will answer the call to live an extreme Christian life? Let me ask
you the following questions to help you answer this question:

Are you ready:

1. To be one of those who demonstrates EXTREME BELIEF in Jesus Christ?

By *Extreme Belief*, I don't mean believing Jesus for
things that are simple and commonplace. No, I'm talking
about *"beyond-the-norm"* belief.

Christianity began with *extreme belief*
when the angel Gabriel came to Mary and
said, "You are going to give birth to a child.
The child is going to be conceived of God…"

> I love the part of our Christian life where God challenges us to grow and to go to a new level in Him. We all need it.

*And in the sixth month the angel
Gabriel was sent from God unto a
city of Galilee, named Nazareth, To
a virgin espoused to a man whose
name was Joseph, of the house of*

David; and the virgin's name was Mary. And the angel came in unto her, and said, "Hail, thou that art highly favoured, the Lord is with thee: blessed art thou among women." And when she saw him, she was troubled at his saying, and cast in her mind what manner of salutation this should be. And the angel said unto her, "Fear not, Mary: for thou hast found favour with God. And, behold, thou shalt conceive in thy womb, and bring forth a son, and shalt call his name JESUS. He shall be great, and shall be called the Son of the Highest: and the Lord God shall give unto him the throne of his father David: And he shall reign over the house of Jacob for ever; and of his kingdom there shall be no end."

Then said Mary unto the angel, "How shall this be, seeing I know not a man?"

And the angel answered and said unto her, "The Holy Ghost shall come upon thee, and the power of the Highest shall overshadow thee: therefore also that holy thing which shall be born of thee shall be called the Son of God. And, behold, thy cousin Elisabeth, she hath also conceived a son in her old age: and this is the sixth month with her, who was called barren. For with God nothing shall be impossible."

And Mary said, "Behold the handmaid of the Lord; be it unto me according to thy word." And the angel departed from her.
(Luke 1:26-33)

Now, if God came to us and announced that He was about to do something major, most of us would ask a million questions like "How's that going to happen?" "What about this?" or "What about that?" Do you know what happens when you do that? You nullify the miracle.

> If you believe for extreme things, you will be highly blessed and favored by the Lord.

Mary simply said, "Okay...be it unto me just like you said..." Talk about extreme belief! I can just see the angels in heaven turning to one another saying, "My God, did you hear that? She BELIEVES..."

What a far cry that is from how most Christians live today. We have a hard time believing God for anything, and that's why people don't do exploits for Him anymore. Would to God that He would hear the same response from us that Mary gave, "Be it unto me just like You want, Lord. I trust You, and I'm willing to do whatever You want me to do!" Take it from Mary. If you believe for extreme things, you will be highly blessed and favored by the Lord.

Never Too Young Or Too Old

Let me tell you about an extreme friend of mine named George. He's a businessman who got saved at an age when most people are thinking about retiring. George never bought the excuse that he's too old or that he hasn't been saved long enough to do anything for God. Instead, he went to work. Doing what, you might ask?

He began broadcasting the Gospel via television into the homes of over 300 million Muslims in the Middle East. Not only that, but George is taking the Gospel stories and bringing them to life with actors and actresses who speak Arabic. As a result, in nations where it is against the law to preach the Gospel, Muslims can now turn on the television in the privacy of their own homes and watch Jesus preach, heal the sick, and perform miracles! And they're hearing the proclamation of the Gospel through the shed blood of Jesus Christ! How incredible!

George is believing and doing extreme things for God. He's doing things that few people would ever dream of doing. And Satan hates him for it. But God *loves* him for it!

> The Lord is looking for those who will go beyond the baby diaper stage of Christianity.

How To Experience The Fourth Man

If you're faith is being severely tested, draw strength and encouragement from the story of the three Hebrew children. They took a radical stand for God when they defied the king's order by refusing to bow down and worship Nebuchadnezzar's golden image. They even went so far as to tell King Nebuchadnezzar that God was able to deliver them from the fiery furnace.

> *Shadrach, Meshach, and Abednego, answered and said to the king, "O Nebuchadnezzar, we are not careful to answer thee in this matter. If it be so, our God whom we serve is able to deliver us from the burning fiery furnace, and he will deliver us out of thine hand, O king. But if not, be it known unto thee, O king, that we will not serve thy gods, nor worship the golden image which thou hast set up."*
> *(Daniel 3:16-18)*

When Nebuchadnezzar heard their reply, he became so infuriated that he commanded the furnace to be heated seven times hotter than it had been. You know the story. The three Hebrew children were thrown into the fiery furnace. The fire was so hot that it instantly killed those who threw them into the furnace.

Nebuchadnezzar looked into the furnace and got the surprise of his life! He saw the three Hebrew children walking through the fire with a fourth man: a man whose appearance was like that of the son of God! They were, of course, unharmed by the flames.

Oh, how God blesses extreme belief! My friend, you're never going to experience the fourth man in the fire unless you go into the fire. You're never going to accomplish great things for God unless you're willing to step out and believe Him for the impossible.

> You're never going to accomplish great things for God unless you're willing to believe Him for the impossible.

143

It's one thing to believe God to heal a headache. It's quite another to believe Him to heal cancer. It's one thing to believe God to work a miracle in someone else's life. It is quite another to believe God to work a miracle in your own life. It's easy to believe Him when things are going great. It's quite another thing to believe Him in the midst of a severe trial or storm.

I love the part of our Christian life where God challenges us to grow and go to a new level in Him. I need it. You need it. We all need it.

Jesus was constantly challenging the disciples to take them to another level. Can you just imagine the disciples complaining to each other about how much they had to walk or the length of their workday? As they're wiping the dust off their feet, tending their blisters and thinking about taking it easy, He tells them to heal the sick, cast out demons, and raise the dead. What an extreme Savior! And what pleases Him is when we demonstrate extreme belief in Him.

Are you ready:

2. To be one of those who is willing to be known for your EXTREME BEHAVIOR in Jesus Christ?

By extreme behavior, I'm referring to how you conduct yourself, both inwardly and outwardly.

When Paul told Timothy, *"Let no man despise your youth but be an example of the believers in word, in conversation, in charity, in spirit, in purity"* (I Timothy 4:12), he was saying, "Timothy, everybody else lives 'down here.' I want you to live 'up here.' Be an example. Set the pace. Show everybody else how they're supposed to live."

> God wants us to be extreme in how we conduct ourselves, both inwardly and outwardly.

Jesus constantly disturbed people with His extreme behavior. Imagine the scene that transpired when He taught the Sermon on the Mount (Matthew 5). The disciples were all seated around the beautiful hillside overlooking the Sea of Galilee. They had no idea what Jesus was about to say. They'd seen Him turn the water into wine, heal the sick and raise the dead.

They were hoping that He would establish an earthly kingdom and deliver them from Roman tyranny. After all, they'd seen Him work mighty miracles that no one else could perform. This was Jesus who turned the water into wine. Who opened blind eyes. Who raised Lazarus from the dead.

They must have gone into shock when He told them, "Hey guys, do you want to be great in My kingdom? Become a servant. Love your enemies. Pray for them. Turn the other cheek…" How contrary this was to what they'd previously been taught, *an eye for an eye and a tooth for a tooth.* This was *extreme behavior.*

I want to share with you in depth three practical areas where you need to be extreme in your behavior. I recommend that at the end of each week, you examine yourself by asking, "Have I been extreme in these areas of my life this week?"

Are you extreme in your *life?*

I don't know about you, but I refuse to live in that safe, comfortable territory where so many Christians live. I want to be someone the Lord can count on to step out of the boat and believe Him for the impossible.

What I'm sharing with you is the difference between living a mundane, lazy, good-for-nothing Christian life, and doing something for God. One day, every single one of us is going to be held accountable for what we did with our lives. You have the opportunity to make a major difference in this world, even if you're just a dear old grandma.

A person who's extreme in his life is extreme in his behavior. Philippians 2:15 says that we are to be *"blameless and pure, children of God without fault in a crooked*

> You have the opportunity to make a major difference in this world, even if you're just a dear old grandma.

and depraved generation in which you shine like the stars of the universe."(NIV)

As believers, our lives are supposed to shine forth Jesus in the midst of this dark and sinful world. How? By being blameless, pure, and holy in our behavior.

> *But like the Holy One who called you, be holy yourselves also in all your behavior.*
> *(1 Peter 1:15, NASB)*

To be holy in all your behavior means that you are set apart from the world. You act differently. You do different things. You look different. You dress different. You live different. Why? Because you ARE different!

That's why we're admonished in Romans 12:2 to *"be not conformed to this world: but be ye transformed by the renewing of your mind, that ye may prove what is that good, and acceptable, and perfect, will of God."*

I love the Phillips translation of Romans 12:2 which says, *"Do not let this world put you into it's mold..."*

"Do not let." This means don't allow or permit. The world will try to put you into its mold. But you have a choice in the matter. You can decide to not allow it. Instead, determine that you're going to renew your mind by the Word of God and the power of the Holy Spirit. As you do, it will transform your life, and even change your future!

"Because You Were Faithful With A Biscuit..."

Let me share another story with you about extreme living. When I got saved, I got radically saved. Overnight, I went from being a cussing drug addict to saying things like, "Glory to God! Praise the Lord, may I please have a sprite?"

I became a "holy roller." I was so on fire for God, I drove everybody around me crazy. I didn't have to tell any of my unsaved buddies goodbye – they all left me. They just couldn't stand to be around me anymore.

Soon after I got saved, God put me in a place called Outreach Ministries of Alabama (OMA), and from there I went to Bible school. When I entered OMA, they made me the cook. It was the lowest position for the lowest man on the totem pole.

As the cook, I had to get up earlier than everyone else and cook the meals. One day, a huge sack of flour was donated to the ministry. Unfortunately, many of the donations that are given to thesse types of ministries are not fit to be given to dogs. That was the case with this flour. I opened up the sack of white flour and noticed that it had black specs in it. So I scooped some up, put it on the table, rubbed it out and all the black specs started moving around. The flour was infested with bugs. Thousands of them.

So I called all the guys in and said, "Guys, I know your favorite breakfast is biscuits and gravy (because they could eat until they exploded). We've got all the ingredients, but here's the hitch. Here's the flour – look – it's infested with bugs." I showed them the flour with the bugs. "You've got a choice. Either I make the biscuits and gravy with this bug-infested flour, or we have cereal…" Every single guy – 15 in total – said to fix the biscuits. So I did.

Now remember, what I'm sharing with you has everything to do with being *extreme with your life*. I'm talking about being holy in your behavior. About how you walk, talk, think and act. About your obedience.

One of the rules in the house was no eating between meals. After breakfast was over, as I was washing the dishes and cleaning up the kitchen, I suddenly realized that I had not eaten breakfast. And I was hungry. I looked over at the oven and saw two remaining biscuits. I walked over, grabbed one of the biscuits, put it in my mouth and bit into it. As soon as I bit into it, a cloud came over me. And the Spirit of the Lord said to me, "What are you doing?" And I said, "Jesus, I'm eating breakfast." And He said, "Breakfast is over."

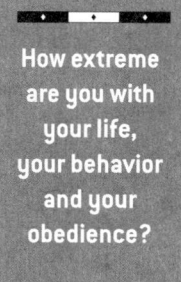

How extreme are you with your life, your behavior and your obedience?

Now remember, before I was saved, I was a criminal. I had been a drug addict. I stole and had been doing anything that I wanted to do for years. I was a "free" man. Now, here I was standing in the kitchen with half a biscuit in my mouth, having this conversation with the Lord. I took the biscuit out of my mouth and put it down. I had already swallowed some of it, and I started falling under conviction.

For the next two weeks, I carried the heaviest burden that a man could carry. I couldn't sing in chapel. I couldn't worship God. I couldn't lift my hands in worship because I had broken a rule. I felt horrible.

Finally, after the burden was too much to bear, I realized that I needed to confess. Most people think that this is absolutely ridiculous, but not to a man of God. I walked into the staff office and said to the director, "I need to talk to you about something." Now, they were accustomed to hearing stories like this, "Before I came to OMA, I murdered a man," or "I robbed a bank..." So the director was bracing himself for the worst.

I started to weep and said, "Scottie, remember two weeks ago, when I cooked those biscuits and gravy with all those bugs in it?" "Yes. I remember. I was there." "After breakfast, I realized that I had not eaten. I looked over at the stove, and on top of the stove were two biscuits. I walked over to the stove after breakfast when everyone was gone, grabbed a biscuit, bit down and I ate it..."

> The Lord knew that because I was faithful to be obedient with the biscuit, that I would also be faithful with the mantle of His glory.

Scottie was sitting at his desk trying not to crack up. After all, he expected to hear a horrifying confession, and here I was confessing to eating a biscuit. There was a long pause. Then Scottie composed himself and said to me, "Let me tell you something, Steve Hill. You have broken the rules. You've spent your life breaking rules and laws. I'm going to teach you something today. You're going to learn that the Christian life is not like that. Christianity has rules and regulations, and if you're going to be a man of God, you are going to have to learn how to follow the teaching of the Word of God and the Holy Ghost. I'm going to discipline you..."

He then gave me a little brush that you clean finger nails with and told me to go to the kitchen and scrub every square inch of the floor. He said, "I want you to move the stove, refrigerator, and every appliance, and scrub this floor until it's spotless. Do you understand?" I answered, "Yes, I do." And I remember that as I was on my hands and knees scrubbing that floor, the Spirit of God came upon me and said, "Steve, I love you. If you will be faithful in the little things, I will bless you with big things."

Remember, I'm sharing with you about *extreme life*. Extreme obedience. Years went by. Then, in 1995, God chooses to place me in what some say was the greatest revival since Azusa Street. Right in the center of it. Many people said, "You are at the tip of the arrow of the revival, Steve." Anytime someone came in from CNN, The New York Times, 20/20 or the like, they all wanted to talk to me because I was the evangelist. And the Lord knew that because I was faithful to be obedient with the biscuit, that I would also be faithful with the mantle of His glory.

That's why when CNN asked me, "What's it like to be a famous, international evangelist?" I looked into the camera, burst into tears and said, "Famous? Famous? I'm nothing but a drug addict saved by grace. It's all because of Jesus." The cameraman was visibly moved. The producer began to weep. The Spirit of God fell into the room and the producer said, "Cut. Cut. Cut. Reverend, we can't put this on CNN. It's too emotional!"

You see, God knew that I would be faithful to lift up Jesus, not myself. He remembered how I was faithful with the biscuit.

My friend, God is expecting you to start being extreme in your behavior, first in the "little things..."

Are you extreme in *love?*

He is also expecting you to be extreme in your love. It's not an option; it's a command.

And the second is like, namely this, Thou shalt love thy neighbour as thyself. There is none other commandment greater than these. (Mark 12:31)

It's easy to read in the Bible where Jesus commands us to love one another, but wait until you have to put it into practice! Have you ever had someone irritate you? I have. Frequently. But I have learned the importance of putting extreme love into practice when people irritate me.

One time, my wife and I were planting a church and a Teen Challenge Center in Belarus, Russia. We had moved into the ghettos to plant this church, and it was tough.

There was a popular Russian reporter who hated my guts. He took my book *Stone Cold Heart* and editorially ripped it to shreds, even though he had never met me or spoken to me. He spread it all over the newspaper that our ministry was a cult. The work that we were doing for God was viewed as evil because of him.

As a result of his negative publicity, the KGB was after us. They'd pull us in, line us all up, take our passports, and try to intimidate us. On top of that, the mafia was always on my back. They control everything in Russia.

The Lord spoke to me one day about how to change this reporter. *He showed me how to love my enemy.* I went to one of my staff and told him to find that reporter and tell him, "Steve Hill appreciates the energy and the quality that you put forth in your writing, and he wants to know if you'd be open and willing to be hired as one of our translators to translate our English material into Russian..."

Do you want the favor and the blessing of God upon your life? Then learn to be extreme in your love.

Do you know what happened? The reporter turned around and started translating our ministry materials. He was a phenomenal translator. And guess what else happened. The tone of all his articles about us changed.

I'm talking about extreme love that blesses those who speak evil about us.

But I say unto you, Love your enemies, bless them that curse you, do good to them that hate you, and pray for them which despitefully use you, and persecute you. (Matthew 5:44)

I'm talking about an extreme love that speaks a soft answer that turns away wrath.

A soft answer turneth away wrath: but grievous words stir up anger. (Proverbs 15:1)

Do you want the favor and the blessing of God upon your life? Then learn to be extreme in your love!

Are you extreme in your *labor?*

Let me give you a secret on how to be successful in your workplace: don't work for your boss; work for Jesus! Of course, your boss is your authority. But when you're working to please Jesus rather than man, the Lord will bless you and turn situations around for you.

And whatsoever ye do, do it heartily, as to the Lord, and not unto men. (Colossians 3:23)

Whatsoever thy hand findeth to do, do it with thy might; for there is no work, nor device, nor knowledge, nor wisdom, in the grave, whither thou goest. (Ecclesiastes 9:10)

You see, when you're working for Jesus and your boss cusses you out, he's cussing at Jesus. And because you're representing the Lord on your job and doing your best to work for Him, you take the problem to Him in prayer. You pray, "Jesus, I'm doing my very best. I'm working overtime. I'm not asking for anything

> It was more than just a job. It was a mission field.

in return. I'm doing everything I can, and this man keeps cussing at me and slamming me. I'm doing this for You, Jesus. Help me to be a light here in this workplace."

This reminds me of a time when Jeri and I were first starting out in the ministry. We didn't have any money at the time, so we had to do some tent making. Jeri got a job in a library working with the blind and handicapped. The blind would call in and want her to send sexually explicit brail books. The stuff was filthy. Jeri, being the on-fire Christian that she was, just couldn't in good conscious send out pornographic material. So when someone would call up requesting something filthy, she'd send them something like *Bambi* instead. It didn't take long before her boss wrote her up. But she stood her ground and told them that she just couldn't do it. Then she started a prayer meeting at the library, and women began to come early to the meeting to get saved.

Sure, it was secular income, and we needed the money. But it was more than just a job to Jeri. It was a mission field. She was doing it as unto the Lord. Her labor was extreme.

Let me clarify here that I'm not talking about being ridiculous by doing stuff your boss won't let you do. But, Jeri was open with her boss and told her why she couldn't do what she was asking her to do. Jeri ended up becoming friends with her boss. One time, we even laid hands on her and prayed for her.

Whether you're a housewife raising your children, a college student on a work-study program, a business professional, a waitress, a minister of the Gospel – whatever your occupation and whatever your hand finds to do, do it with all your might as unto the Lord. Be extreme in your labor, and watch God bless the work of your hands!

Are you ready:

3. To be one of those who is a recipient of EXTREME BLESSINGS from Jesus Christ?

The Lord loves kissing faithfulness.

Some Christians are absolutely mind-boggled when the Lord blesses them. People come up to me and say stuff like, "Pastor, you're never going to believe what's happening. I've been seeking God and tithing, and I got a raise. I'm making double what I was making before I started attending Heartland!" They act shocked when God blesses them.

There's something I've learned about the Lord over the years: He loves kissing faithfulness! As you are faithful to the Lord, you position yourself to be a recipient of His blessings in every area of your life.

Let's look at just a few of His awesome promises about extreme blessings.

Your 'Farm', which represents your real estate and livelihood:

> *Yea, the LORD shall give that which is good; and our land shall yield her increase.*
> *(Psalm 85:12)*

Your Family:

> *For I will pour water upon him that is thirsty, and floods upon the dry ground: I will pour my spirit upon thy seed, and my blessing upon thine offspring.* *(Isaiah 44:3)*

Your Finances:

> *Bring ye all the tithes into the storehouse, that there may be meat in mine house, and prove me now herewith, saith the LORD of hosts, if I will not open you the windows of heaven, and pour you out a blessing, that there shall not be room enough to receive it. And I will rebuke the devourer for your sakes, and he shall not destroy the fruits of your ground; neither shall your vine cast her fruit before the time in the field, saith the LORD of hosts. And all nations shall call you blessed: for ye shall be a delightsome land, saith the LORD of hosts.* (Malachi 3:10-12)

Your Future:

> *But as it is written, Eye hath not seen, nor ear heard, neither have entered into the heart of man, the things which God hath prepared for them that love him.* (I Corinthians 2:9)

What A Life!

What a life! We get to be recipients of His extreme blessings upon this earth, and then we get heaven, too! This is why Christians should be slightly annoying to be around.

As God's people, we should be saying stuff like, "Glory to God!" "What did you say?" "I said, 'Glory to God!'" "What does that mean?" "Oh, He receives all the praise for everything going on in my life…" "Well, what's going on in your life?" "Well, praise God, I just got a huge raise! Not only that, but He recently healed my mother of terminal cancer! Thank You, Jesus…"

My friend, He *wants* to pour out extreme blessings upon you. As you're faithful in your life, your labor, and your love, you position yourself to be a recipient of His extreme blessings.

Are you ready:

4. To be one of those who radiates with EXTREME BEAUTY as the Bride of Jesus Christ?

> Are you more in love with Jesus today than you were back when you were first saved?

The moment a bride-to-be gets engaged, her life changes. Overnight, her priorities are rearranged and she becomes focused upon one primary goal: to be wed to the man she loves. Months of planning and hard work will follow, all for that great and glorious wedding day.

It's amazing what a bride will go through to prepare herself for that big day. She may go on a diet. Exercise. Shop for days and spend hundreds, possibly thousands of dollars on just the right dress – a dress that she's only going to wear once. She'll buy matching shoes, and new jewelry. She may go to a tanning salon. Get a makeover. Get a spa treatment. Get her hair and nails done. The list goes on and on.

Why does she go to all that trouble? Because she's head-over-heels in love with her bridegroom, and when she walks down that aisle, she wants to be the most beautiful, radiant bride that her beloved has ever seen!

My wife, Jeri, was an absolutely gorgeous bride. As I was writing this portion about the Bride of Christ, I pulled out a picture of Jeri that was taken on our wedding day, more than twenty-five years ago. As I gazed at her beauty and reminisced about our wedding day, my heart was overwhelmed.

I turned to Jeri and said, "Honey, you were absolutely ravishing on our wedding day, but you're ten thousand times more ravishing today. You're incredible – your holiness, your love for the Lord, your physical and inner beauty...everything about you, babe, is awesome. I was madly in love with you when we first married, and I'm even more in love with you today..."

Christ and His Bride

We know that the relationship between a husband and wife is but an earthly picture of the relationship between Christ and His Bride. The Bible speaks of this relationship as *a great mystery.*

> *Husbands, love your wives, even as Christ also loved the church, and gave himself for it; That he might sanctify and cleanse it with the washing of water by the word, That he might present it to himself a glorious church, not having spot, or wrinkle, or any such thing; but that it should be holy and without blemish... This is a great mystery: but I speak concerning Christ and the church.* (Ephesians 5:25-27,32)

What might Jesus say about your relationship with Him today, compared to the time when you first gave your life to Him? Has your relationship with Him grown and flourished over time? Are you more in love with Him today than you were back then?

A Day Worth Living For

> There's a day coming that you should be living for, longing for and preparing for every single day of your life.

Beloved, there's a day coming that you should be living for, longing for, and preparing for, each and every day of your life. It's the day when you see Jesus, your heavenly Bridegroom, face-to-face. It's the day that you are ushered in to the Marriage Supper of the Lamb to be with Him for all eternity.

Have you ever seriously thought about that day when you stand before the Lord? You should. I don't just think about it – I *live* with a continual awareness of the fact that one day soon I am going to stand before Him. This awareness motivates me, and affects my decisions, my actions and how I live my life.

Of this one thing I'm certain. When I stand before my Lord and see Him face-to-face, I want to hear Him say, "Steve, the day you gave your life to Me – when I washed your sins away, gave you a new heart and took you as My very own – you were so beautiful to Me. But today you shine with a radiance that's ten thousand times more beautiful because you've lived holy and kept your garments clean ever since you've known Me.

"There's no greater love you could have shown Me, than to have laid down your life for My beloved Bride the way that you did. Son, that's why millions of people are in heaven today... because of your love and faithfulness to Me. And Steve, every single soul that you've won is a reward to Me for My suffering. *Thank you* for living your life for Me.

"You were faithful and obedient through the good times and the hard times, whether skies were sunny or storm clouds raged. You remained true to Me and My Word. You preached My Word without compromise. You endured. You overcame. You ran your race well and finished your course. Well done, My faithful son.

"I have so much in store for you, and it will take all of eternity to show you how much I love you. Come, let me show you the great reward that I have waiting for you..."

My friend, that's the day I'm living for. How about you?

The Prepared Bride

As Christians, we are a chosen people. He has called us out of darkness into His marvelous light. We are born of His Spirit and adopted into His family. God is now our Father, and Jesus is our Lord, our Savior, and our heavenly Bridegroom.

One day soon, He is coming back to take us to live with Him forever. The Word of God gives us a glimpse of that fast approaching day, and instructs us how to prepare for it:

> *"Let us rejoice and be glad and give him glory! For the wedding of the Lamb has come, and **his bride has made herself ready**. Fine linen, bright and clean, was given her to wear." (Fine linen stands for the righteous acts of the saints.)*
>
> *Then the angel said to me, "Write: 'Blessed are those who are invited to the wedding supper of the Lamb!'" And he added, "These are the true words of God."   (Revelation 19:7-9, NIV)*

His bride has made herself ready! No bride shows up for her own wedding without making herself ready. How much more should we, the Bride of Christ, make every effort to prepare ourselves to be forever united with our heavenly Bridegroom!

How do you prepare yourself for the Lord? By living separate from the world. By keeping your garments clean. By living a holy and a pure life. By keeping your first love passion for Him. By living an extreme Christian life.

It takes effort to be holy and to live for God. But as His Bride, you wouldn't want to live any other way. Pleasing Him is your highest goal and greatest delight. Why? Because you're deeply in love with Him!

This, my friend, is the secret to radiating with ***extreme beauty!***

It's Time

> The greatest of all adventures awaits those who choose to live a life of EXTREME CHRISTIANITY.

Time. Have you ever noticed that the older you get, the faster it seems to fly by? On the one hand, I love getting older. At this stage in my life, I know who I am and where I'm going. I've gained wisdom and seasoning over the years. I'm more focused than ever on what God has called me to do, and I wouldn't want to trade this season of my life for anything.

But on the other hand, I'm extremely conscious of the fact that the clock is ticking and I only have twenty-five to thirty years of ministry left. And that bothers me because there's so much work to do for the Kingdom of God and so little time to do it.

The fact of the matter is, no one knows how much time he has on earth, nor do any of us know when Jesus will return. This is why the Word instructs us to make the most of every day and every opportunity that the Lord gives us:

> Look carefully then how you walk! **Live purposefully and worthily and accurately,** not as the unwise and witless, but as wise (sensible, intelligent people), **Making the very most of the time [buying up each opportunity],** because the days are evil. Therefore do not be vague and thoughtless and foolish, but understanding **and firmly grasping what the will of the Lord is.**
> (Ephesians 5:15-17, Amplified)

How I love that! *Live purposefully and worthily and accurately...as wise...making the very most of the time...*

Let's not forget these Words of Jesus, *"Behold, I am coming soon! My reward is with me, and I will give to everyone according to what he has done"* (Revelation 22:12).

As I shared with you at the beginning of this study, no matter where you're at in your Christian journey, God has more for you. But it's up to you to go after it. It's up to you to press in and take hold of what He has for you. The Lord wants to do new things in your life, if you'll let Him.

Are you ready to believe Him for great things? To get out of the boat? To take risks? To be radical for Him? To live an extreme Christian life? To take your place in His mighty army? To let the Lord take you places you've never gone before? Are you determined to make your life count for eternity?

If you answer "Yes!" then get ready for the greatest of all adventures, and, on that day when you see Him face-to-face, for the most incredible of all rewards!

Questions For Group Discussion

Here are some questions for discussion that are related to the challenge, *"Are you one of those who will answer the call to live an extreme Christian life?"*

1. How does your life demonstrate EXTREME BELIEF in Jesus Christ?

    _____

    _____

    _____

    _____

2. Are you willing to be known for your EXTREME BEHAVIOR in Jesus Christ?

    *   In your life?

        _____

        _____

        _____

    *   In love?

        _____

        _____

        _____

    *   In your labor?

        _____

        _____

        _____

3. Are you ready to be one of those who is a recipient of EXTREME BLESSING from Jesus Christ?

_____

_____

_____

_____

4. Are you ready to be one of those who radiates with EXTREME BEAUTY as the Bride of Jesus Christ?

_____

_____

_____

_____